PICK – Your System

by

Nicola Kitt

 Publishers. Wilmslow

 HALSTED PRESS a division of **JOHN WILEY & SONS**
New York · Chichester · Brisbane · Toronto

ISBN 1-85058-031-6 (Sigma Press)
ISBN 0-470-20320-X (Halsted Press)

Published by:

SIGMA PRESS
98a Water Lane
Wilmslow
Cheshire U.K.

and

HALSTED PRESS
a Division of John Wiley & Sons Inc,
New York.

Printed by: Interprint, Malta

Distributed by:

U.K., Europe, Africa:
JOHN WILEY & SONS LIMITED
Baffins Lane, Chichester
West Sussex, England

Australia: JOHN WILEY & SONS INC.
GPO Box 859, Brisbane
Queensland 40001 Australia

Trademark

PICK is a registered trademark of Pick Systems Inc.

ACKNOWLEDGEMENTS

I would like to acknowledge all my friends who without exception have been interested, amazed and supportive over this venture – without which I'd never have finished. Many thanks to my extended family who have unreservedly given support, advice and criticism, thanks Dens, Kath, Peter, Una, Andrew, Mark, Paul, Gill, Adrian and Steph.

Also many thanks to:
Chris Winters of Fletcher Compute Services
Phil and Margaret Harris of Cougar Pumps

and last but by no means least Mic Merrison and Bob Burrows, who set me on this path!

This book is dedicated to Steve.

Nicola Kitt, 1986

CONTENTS

Chapter 1

What is an Operating System?

To be able to answer the question "What is an operating system?" it is necessary to examine the skeleton of the computer. This is comprised of a number of electrical components which are known collectively as the hardware. As the skeleton forms the basis for the human body, so the hardware supports and gives the physical realisation of a computer. The computer that we, the users, employ seems far removed from the "bones" of the machine. We have the facilities to produce a profit and loss account at the touch of a button and often without the realisation that these facilities are merely flesh on top of the skeleton. Take away all the fancy functions and the circuitry reappears.

The physical parts of a computer, known as the hardware, include the terminal (going under various aliases such as CRT, VDU, and screen), the disks (both fixed and removable , hard and floppy) where data is stored, and the electronic circuitry which consists mainly of integrated circuits commonly known as "chips". It is these chips which are capable of carrying out the repetitive number crunching that computers are renowned for.

The hardware is fundamentally only capable of the basic arithmetic operations for addition, subtraction and multiplication as well as the logical evaluations for greater than, equal to and less than, represented by the characters $>$, $=$, $<$.

Every computer that is manufactured and sold, whatever its size, shape and purpose is only capable of these basic functions at skeleton level. It is the aim of an operating system to turn the "bones " of the hardware into something that appears to do a lot more than this so that it can be used by the ordinary user, even the novice.

The operating system is part of a collection of software found in a computer. This is the second part of a computer or the non- physical portion. Software is a curious commodity, as it appears to be invisible when resident on a

1

computer but fills pages of popular magazines in the form of space invader program listings for the BBC micro! The different types of software programs cover a large and varied range of tasks and problems. In fact anything which includes padding on top of the hardware, such as an arcade game like space invaders or a stock taking system is software. Software is comprised of programs containing instructions which are performed by the machine. The programs use data which may already be stored permanently within the machine either in parts of the circuitry or on magnetic disks and tapes; this sort of storage medium may be read as and when the data is required. Software covers many aspects of computing, which can be categorised to include:

> Operating systems
> Assemblers
> Compilers
> Utilities
> Application software.

All of these categories of software have different areas of expertise, but they all rely on the operating system software (often know as systems software) to form a cornerstone on which the different types of programs are built, resulting in the different categories of software.

It is intended in this chapter to concentrate on the category of operating systems software. This consists of special programs which control the running and internal organisation of the computer once the human user has relinquished control. The system software co-ordinates the different parts of the hardware in order to get the requested job completed. The operating system is usually the only piece of software to deal directly with the hardware responsible for obtaining mathematical answers.

Systems software is normally provided by the supplier of the computer hardware as it is usually integral to the operation of the machine. Very often systems software is the part of the computer that a user is least aware of. A user will be far more aware and interested in the profit (or loss!) figures coming out of an accounting program than how data is handled internally by the machine from which the results are being obtained.

Although the user may not realise it, the operating system is as important to the operation of the machine as the hardware itself.

Why do we Need an Operating System?

An operating system is the interface between the computer user and the machine.

The actual electronic circuitry which does the processing requires all its data and information in sequences of 0's and 1's, this is known as binary. Binary has two possible digits (0 or 1), a single binary digit is known as a BIT. Bits are stored and processed by means of electronics. The data which a human deals with is very rarely exclusively in 1's and 0's. Data as we know it are long lists of names and addresses, parts in stock, order numbers, clients' credit ratings and other such information. If a computer is to handle this data and manipulate it as we request, it must be received by the hardware coded in binary form, as this is the way chips store and process information most easily.

Not only must the data be coded in binary but also the instructions which make up a program; in order for the computer to know how the data is to be processed. To use a computer in a skeleton state would involve translating everything into 0's and 1's and feeding in the binary strings. In addition, a knowledge of how the circuitry performs basic mathematical functions and operations would be necessary in order to get any results from the machine. It goes without saying that any results would also be in binary. A simple request to add two numbers together would look something like this:

```
00111010
01100000
00000000
01000111
00111010
01100001
00000000
10000000
00110010
01100010
00000000
```

A complex procedure which only the fanatical would use! So in order to make computers available to people who don't think in terms of 1 and 0, the operating system was invented.

The Evolution of the Operating System.

The operating system started its evolutionary path in a small way. It became very tedious to continue inputting sequences of 0's and 1's in the correct order, so operations that were used regularly by many people were created as functions. In the case of the above example the word ADD would have been created to instruct the operating system to fetch the program ADD (as seen in Figure 1.1), and place it in main memory, being a sort of middleman. The processor could then execute the program bit by bit.

Gradually all the common functions, such as adding two numbers together, fetching data from a storage location or having something printed on the line printer, became routines. The new vocabulary of the operating system, although time saving, was still not giving the programmer enough scope, so new languages appeared: including BASIC, FORTRAN, COBOL,

ALGOL and many many more. These use **English-type** words which are translated by large specially written pieces of software into the necessary 0's and 1's (apart from the already coded functions in the operating system). The translation programs are known as compilers, a software category mentioned earlier.

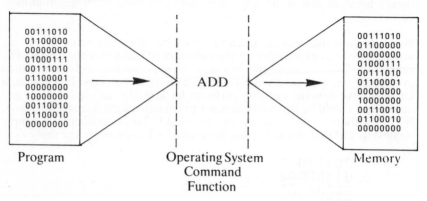

| Program | Operating System Command Function | Memory |

Figure 1.1

The programmer would select the required translation program and read it into the computer memory and his own program would then be read in for the compiler to translate into 1's and 0's. Once translated the program was compiled and would be run. Whenever extra data was needed these compiled programs would stop and type out a message on the printer; all processing ceased until a reply was given. If the programmer was out to lunch when the stop occurred then the computer would just sit and wait wasting processing time until an answer was received. The stop may have been for a tape of data to be loaded; the computer needed human help as it did not have the ability to know where data was or where to get it from.

Such dependence on human intervention only seemed to waste valuable computing time. As a result the operating system began to undertake some of the programmer's duties, such as locating the required compiler from tape or disk storage, feeding data into programs as necessary and monitoring the performance of programs. Before long the operating system was resident in main memory on a permanent basis. Over the years more and more functions and tasks have been added to the operating system.

At this stage in the evolutionary process of the operating system, the touch of a button would read a compiler into main memory, read and translate the program and place the translation onto magnetic backing storage. The operating system then takes over from the compiler, reading the program from storage into main memory allowing the program to run, printing any results on the printer or sending them back to the terminal the request came from. Programs are given permission by the operating system to do their work, but if a program makes a fatal error, or simply runs for too long, the operating system then throws it out to make way for the next program waiting to be processed.

This is viewed very similarly in concept to waiting to pay for groceries at a supermarket. Very often a whole queue of people are kept waiting; the cashier is idle while someone goes to look for the price of a tin of peaches. The whole system is doing nothing. A computer is no different: while the operating system goes to look for some data programs are queuing up and the processor is idle, waiting for the operating system to return with the information. The machine is kept waiting a long time for data to be fetched from storage, for replies by its human masters or for the really slow printer to finish outputting a report. All this time the processor is idle when it could be processing thousands of instructions each second.

The next stage of the development of the operating system was to process more than one task at a time. While one job was waiting for some data from backing storage the second program could start to be processed. If one program has to wait, another program can make use of the facilities that would otherwise be lying idle. This is known as *multiprogramming*. Of course this is much more complicated and takes up much more memory,

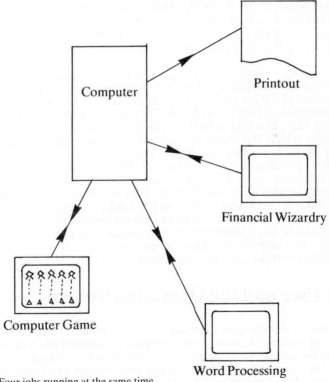

Figure 1.2 Four jobs running at the same time.

making the need for bigger memory capacity. The expansion of the operating system has been possible due to the falling costs of very large memory chips.

All of the tasks shown in Figure 1.2: playing a computer game , a secretary doing word processing, the accountant doing financial forecasting and the printer printing a report, appear to be working at the same time. This is only possible because the operating system has been developed and expanded so that it can switch rapidly between different programs, ensuring that none has to wait long before getting its turn. If we look at the supermarket check-out again, an assistant has now gone off to find out the price of the offending un-priced article so, the next person in the queue starts to have their basket of goods processed, but as soon as the price for customer one's goods is found and given to the cashier, customer two's adding up is stopped, and a note of the total is kept. Customer one's basket of goods is then finished. So, instead of being idle,the cashier has managed to process half of customer two's goods reducing the size of the queue. This is exactly what the operating system does: rather than lying idle it switches to another user's request while the original job is waiting for some more information. This cuts down the amount of time a user has to wait for a job to be processed. The system program which controls this type of function is very large and complex and is not usually found on micro computers, which normally only cater for a single user. An operating system with the ability to process more than one task at a time has the ability to *time-share* or *multi-process*.

As operating systems became larger and more complex a new task (a job in its own right) emerged called systems programming. Systems programmers need to know the internal workings of a computer and the way in which the operating system goes about its job. They are are exclusively concerned with keeping the operating system working and running correctly. Any new functions which the computer manufacturer provides are installed and tested by them so that any errors can be eliminated without the entire computer grinding to a shuddering halt. They also help the machine to run efficiently, not unlike a mechanic tuning a high performance car, enabling the driver to obtain the best from the vehicle. While they are found mainly in mainframe installations such as for banking, insurance and retailing, minicomputers may also have some systems work, but usually only by one person who is also a programmer. A mainframe is by far the most expensive machine to maintain and keep up and running, so it is in this type of installation that the systems programmer is the most cost-effective.

The User and the Operating System

By sitting at any computer terminal, the user is in fact face to face with the operating system. As soon as the terminal is switched on, a cursor is there waiting for a response in the form of a recognisable command, which will be part of its vocabulary. More often than not; in order to engage the machine in conversation a password has to be typed in.

The following sequence of events has been known to take place first thing in the morning.

GOOD MORNING

What is your password ?

The bleary eyed user is met with this cheering message and the blinking cursor. The next step is to enter the correct password at the prompt provided. On entering the correct password and hitting the 'Return' key, communication with the operating system is taking place. To check that the entered password is valid and correct the password received has to be input to the hardware for it to perform a basic arithmetic function, (in this case an equality evaluation) to see if the string of characters input as the password corresponds with a pattern of characters already stored in a specific place by the operating system. The sequence of activities is something like this:

"Is the input password equal to stored password ?"

"If YES pass message to operating system to be output to sending terminal"

WELCOME TO ABC COMPUTER

"Have all the stored passwords been looked at?"

"If NO look at the next password"

"If YES output:

INVALID PASSWORD TRY AGAIN —

While this conversation is taking place communication with the operating system is taking place and utilising the basic functions that an operating system performs.

The Functions of an Operating System

By looking at how the operating system came into being ,and why we need it, the major characteristics of such a piece of software have been found to be:

Storage

Storage can take many forms, all of which are based on saving bits on magnetic surfaces, i.e. hard disk, floppy disk and tape.

This function looks after the storage, retrieval and maintenance of all the data that is held . This data can be of various formats: a program or part of a program; a string of figures relating to an accounting program or perhaps an answer that a program has produced. It is not unlike thinking of a computer as a filing cabinet and the operating system as the secretary in charge of all the filing, fetching and running. The secretary knows the exact location of office documents in the same way the operating system has a method for finding the exact location of a document. You, the boss, still don't know where the file is (in exact terms) but the file can be found by sitting at your desk shouting instructions into a phone or typing at a keyboard!

Control

The operating system in this function takes the responsibility of handling all conditions both expected and unexpected, either by taking some kind of remedial action or by reporting back to the user. In the short 'password' example above, the operating system came back with an error message reporting what it considered to be the most likely cause of error. To have done this it will have looked in the 'password' file (like a secretary) and not found any reference to the required string of characters before sending back a suitable (?) message.

Processing

Any actual calculations using the basic arithmetic functions, as discussed above in the binary ADD example.

Input and output

These two functions take external information and pass it to the operating system for processing and calculation. Input and Output also takes the internal information and converts it back for display in a variety of ways such as on a printer or a screen. It was this Input and Output function which brought the wrong password message from the computer's filing cabinet to the screen. Very much like a secretary actually talking to you...... "I'm sorry but I can't find that file, are you sure it exists ?"

The basic functions briefly outlined will be found within every operating system, however simple, but when several users wish to use a computer at the same time (i.e. the computer acts as a central filing cabinet for more than one person) it supports multiple screens and users and as a result has a more important and complex role to play.

Sequencing of programs

In a computer where there is more than one terminal, the operating system needs the ability to swap programs in and out of the processor in order to give the impression that they are all running concurrently. This allows the available resources to be shared between the users in a fair way so that no-one experiences an unreasonable delay. While doing this the operating system must ensure that the processes of one program are protected from another, in practical terms, making sure that the accounting program and the word processing program do not become muddled! The operating system will also have a priority rating which decides if certain items can jump the queue - the managing director always seems to have a high priority rating!

Filing

This is a feature which developed alongside the advances in computer technology. As storage such as magnetic tapes and magnetic disks became commonplace, the operating system had to have a function which could locate the correct program for the user. For example, a compiler was originally found, selected and loaded into the computer all by human hand, but now it's done completely by computer. As more of the human intervention was eliminated from the operation of a computer so techniques such as filing of programs and data had to be introduced. Not only was filing necessary but so was the efficient and effective retrieval of those files.

Security

The operating system must also guard against any piece of data in the machine being accessed by two or more programs simultaneously. Imagine the following situation: There are two programs, program 1 is waiting for Adrian Wright's address contained in a file of information to be fetched from the disk. While the processor is waiting for that to be done, the operating system starts to process program 2, which requires Adrian's phone number as well as his address. The operating system now has two commands from different programs to fetch the same data for processing. A "Catch 22" situation now ensues - both programs fighting over the same piece of information at the same time. The filing system won't release the information and the programs cannot continue to be processed without it. The operating system has been developed to 'mark' or 'flag' data which has already been requested by a program and to stop it being fetched twice. This type of security makes sure that the stored files are accessed sequentially and not simultaneously. Other types of security taken on by the operating system include password protection for individual high level files, such as personnel records as well as security for 'groups' of users, for example only stock controllers may examine stock related files.

How an operating system works

The basic operating system has these components to support and look after:-

> Input devices
> Output devices
> Storage facilities such as disk or tape
> The memory
> The processor

The components are usually arranged as seen in Figure 1.3, in a small to medium sized computer:

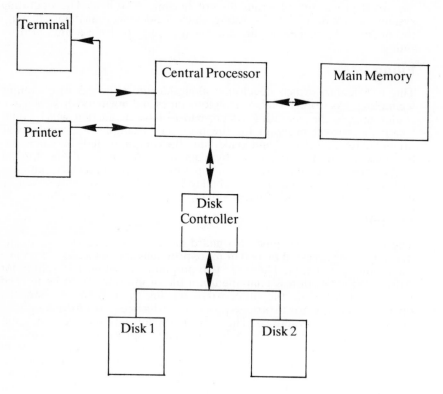

Figure 1.3 Various components of a computer.

To see how all these items are linked together by the computer let's assume that we have a simple program called **CALCULATE**, which has been created and stored on disk. If the program **CALCULATE** is executed, the operating system would respond to the following sequence of events: to start the process the user needs to use an action command with which the operating system is familiar, in this case the word **RUN**. This in turn needs to be followed by the name of the program which is to be processed, in our case **CALCULATE**. This gives the command **RUN CALCULATE**; which when entered is input into the operating system. In this case the operating system has to fetch the program **CALCULATE** from its position in **storage**, using the filing function and place it in the central processing unit (CPU) of the computer. The CPU contains the hardware necessary to carry out the basic functions, the different components can be seen in Figure 1.4.

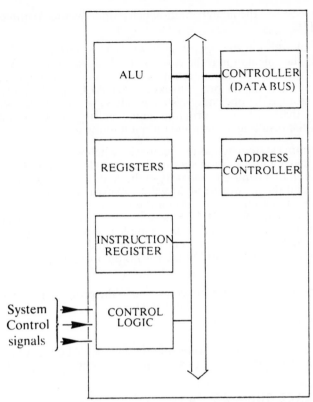

Figure 1.4 The Components of a Central Processing Unit

For the hardware to understand what RUN means the operating system will have undertaken a translation process on behalf of the hardware. The operating system will go to the disk and fetch the program (a program is the only thing that can be RUN) called CALCULATE, it may look something like this when written in the language BASIC.

```
REM THIS IS A CALCULATE PROGRAM
SUM = 28 + 4
PRINT SUM
END
```

The version that the operating system picks up from storage will not look like this. It will be a compiled version, consisting of 0's and 1's, which can be easily understood by the machine .

A computer program must now determine the sources of the data and the destination of the result as well as the operations to be performed.

The operating system takes the entire compiled version of our program and places it in the central processing unit. One instruction at a time will then be

11

executed and processed , the actual addition being done by the Arithmetic Logic Unit (ALU).

During the task of addition the operating system has co-ordinated all the activity to enable the calculation to be carried out. It passed the command to the processor which asked the operating system to fetch CALCULATE from storage. It checked that the program existed. If CALCULATE had not been present on storage the operating system would have output a message telling the user that "no such program name exists". It then, after processing, took the resulting answer and output it to the user.

In effect the operating system acts as an electronic switchboard , requesting information and having information sent to its correct destination. It must also be remembered that computer memory in the central processing unit is only temporary, and the answer to SUM will be overwritten with another program or series of answers. So to obtain the answer to CALCULATE again the command RUN CALCULATE must be re-entered and the whole process repeated. The program used in the example is somewhat limiting as it can only add together the two numbers specified, and so will be of very little (if any) general use. To alter CALCULATE the following steps need to be carried out.

The operating system needs a different command as the program is going to be altered rather that run, so the command will be:

ALTER CALCULATE

Again the operating system orchestrates the finding of CALCULATE on disk and placing it in memory. Another message is now sent to the operating system:

REPLACE SUM = 28 - 4
WITH SUM = 4 - 2

The operating system translates the English-type command and replaces the old calculation. So in memory we have:

REM THIS IS A CALCULATE PROGRAM
SUM = 4 - 2
PRINT SUM
END

and on backing storage we have:

REM THIS IS A CALCULATE PROGRAM
SUM = 28 - 4
PRINT SUM
END

There are now two different versions of CALCULATE. Before the new version can be run and the answer obtained , it has to be filed away to disk so that when the operating system goes to find the program CALCULATE it locates the correct and most up to date version. An operating system will not normally look for the most up to date version of a program in memory. For this reason a command such as **SAVE CALCULATE** is issued. This places the new version safely on disk away from memory where it could easily become overwritten and lost.

Operating Systems Today

All of these facilities, and many more, are provided by a large piece of software. This software stays in the computer all the time and sees each task through, attending to all its particular needs until it is completed. In the days when these programs offered limited facilities and were fairly simplistic they were known as monitors or supervisors, but over the last 10 years they have become increasingly complex and are now known as operating systems. In order for the operating system to perform all its functions it needs to be present in main memory all the time; this has meant that the room left for programs was relatively small, so techniques for managing the remaining memory to the best advantage were developed. This enabled programs bigger than the remaining space to be executed giving a realistically short response time to the user, as well as using the available facilities to the best advantage. See Figure 1.5.

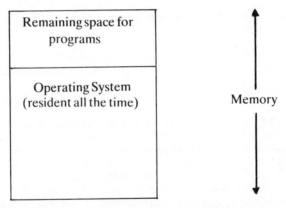

Figure 1.5 Use of remaining space, after operating system is loaded into memory.

This type of operating system can be found on all machines from the smallest home computer to a large IBM mainframe, but these are totally incompatible. It is rather like a street of houses: the homes are designed by different architects and built by a number of local builders. The houses take on their own character by having different coloured bricks, windows of varying shapes and sizes, and of course plots of varying dimensions. All these differences do not detract from the function of the house, or its components: each home will have bedrooms, bathroom, kitchen and living rooms as a minimum. Some may have added extras like a garage, a second bathroom, a study or even a swimming pool. In the same way an operating system has the basic functions: control, processing, input and output, filing and sequencing of programs. Each operating system is built by a different software engineer in a slightly different way, using varying building techniques. All operating systems have the same ultimate goal in mind - a reliable piece of software which controls and sequences the processing of programs, to enable the user to obtain a hopefully understandable response to a question. Operating systems all fulfil this goal to differing extents, but it results in little or no similarity between a personal computer and a mainframe, akin to a terraced house and Buckingham Palace!

Industrial Pressure and Standardisation

The concept of a standard operating system in the computer industry is a relatively new one. In the early 1970's minicomputers were the fastest growing part of the computer industry, each offering their own individually designed, nonstandard proprietary operating systems.

While these manufacturers were developing their hardware and software products each was claiming they should have "The Architect of the Year" award for:

> 1. The best processor using the newest and fastest chips available on the market.

> 2. Implementing a new language (probably invented by one of their staff) which will sweep the world during the next few years.

> 3. New advances made in the design of operating systems.

The operating system was now more user friendly than ever. It had more features than its nearest rival (if it ever had one in the first place) and it goes without saying that the only applications that worked on the machine are the applications produced by the manufacturer! In choosing one of these "award winning systems" from a particular vendor a customer was inextricably tied to that one manufacturer's equipment, since the cost of changing to another totally incompatible system was prohibitive. To change systems would mean re-training staff to use possibly a new language and certainly a new series of operating instructions. Even the accounts clerk would have to learn how the new accounting programs worked.

Why Were New Programs Needed?

All software written for one type of operating system will be tailored to talk to that system in the way that is peculiar to it alone. It's like trying to talk to a Frenchman with only a German dictionary. Some of the words are the same or similar, but they will have different meanings in each of the two languages. In the same way, each "make" of computer has its own language. Try and communicate with it in another language and gross misunderstanding results. As a result, each application has to be developed for each different machine language Since every piece of software is built slightly differently, time is needed to find your way around it. So, software has to be compatible with the operating system. In fact we can take that one stage further and say: as the operating system on a minicomputer is tied to the hardware, the software has to be compatible with that hardware.

In contrast, the 1980's gave way to the introduction of microcomputers. At the last count there were over 200 different microcomputers, but there are merely a handful of operating systems. The microcomputers were dependent upon selling in bulk numbers rather than a few at high prices, and the microcomputer manufacturers could not afford to develop their own operating systems. The operating system began to become standardised. CP/M, MS-DOS, and PC-DOS (enter IBM!) became the standards to be found on any of the microcomputers. As well as the operating systems becoming standardised the actual hardware components became standardised. Micros were powered by chips that were made by the semiconductor specialist "chip" manufacturers such as Intel and Motorola, which resulted in only a small choice of components for the manufacturers. The industry became a series of specialists making one or two components. The actual computer manufacturer bought in the different components from the specialists and put them into a cabinet. It has become too expensive for one company to do all the research, development and manufacture involved in making a computer from scratch. (Except for the blue giant. IBM)

True there are hundreds of microcomputer systems available, but each one is powered by just a handful of standard chips.

Peripherals have become standard to a degree. Floppy disks come in standard sizes (3½", 5¼", and 8") with standard capacities and standard ways of connecting them to the main processor. Returning to the example of a street of family dwelling units, every house had standard components, bricks, window frames, lintels over the doors, and cement. In the same way, computer components are standardised: there are only a limited number of chip vendors or disk suppliers from whom to choose.

The components of an operating system are standardised but the way that they work is different. Copying a file to disk on an IBM-PC will be done differently than on an APPLE II. The same information will be saved in each case but in a totally different way. The IBM-PC can not read the APPLE ll disk and vice versa. Not dissimilar to scientific papers published in German and English - the same information and revelations will be present but the English speaking people will only understand the English version.

So a large to medium sized company that decides to use a micro for word processing, and wants to pass disks between various locations, will have to make sure that all the offices are working with the same operating system, often tying the company to one particular manufacturer and one particular style of software.

Advantages of Standardisation

The standardisation of operating systems allows free movement of data between different machines, rather than each one having its own version of the same programs and data on their incompatible machines. Other advantages of a standard operating system include:

1. The purchaser benefits because he is no longer captive to a single manufacturer. This in effect means that if the purchaser wants or requires a bigger capacity machine with more memory, which the current supplier is unable to provide, he can go to another manufacturer without the expense of having to completely redevelop or indeed purchase new applications software.

2. Those who are involved in the development of application programs benefit as they can offer their products to a wider number of people on a range of differing hardware systems.

3. Indeed, the manufacturers themselves benefit from a more rapid acceptance of their products, and reduced software development costs. A software house is more likely to spend time, money and expertise in developing programs for a widely available operating system than a manufacturer's eccentric state-of-the-art offering.

Chapter 2

Why Consider Pick?

Having studied the functions of a basic operating system, and what it does for the user sitting at a terminal, we now look at the Pick operating system and the problems of integration in the office environment today.

Traditional Operating Systems

The majority of the operating systems on minicomputers were developed for different purposes. For example, the Digital Equipment Corporation (DEC) designed and wrote the DEC VAX series of machines, specifically for scientific, number crunching applications. On the other hand the Pick operating system was designed for the more verbose information retrieval business community. Any operating system will reflect the type of work that the computer is used for. On a scientific machine, the commands and functions are presented in a way that a nuclear physicist will understand and the likes of you or me will not. If an operating system has commands which are difficult to use and understand then the computer becomes difficult to use and understand as this is the only facet of the computer a user will see. An operating system that is not easy to use can result in the computer staying in its packing case, and being a waste of time, space and money. Pick tries to avoid this pitfall and is easy for the novice to learn and use. Pick is designed for business use, and serves the business man better than any other operating system currently available.

An ordinary operating system (such as has been looked at) resembles a single part of a jigsaw - all the other pieces needed to make a complete picture have to be matched and fitted into their correct place, often after several false starts and a lot of trial and error! Having just purchased an Itsy Bitsy 2000, the small businessman needs to do some programming; to do this he needs to select and purchase a compiler, as there is not one with the machine. If he wishes to keep all information centrally in one data-bank another piece of software is needed, all of these "extras" being purchased separately. Building a complete computer system in pieces can be advantageous as it gives a wider choice of products, but the range of choice and the selection process can be hazardous and work against the user. So, the traditional operating system is like the first piece of a jigsaw puzzle, which could end up giving one of many pictures!

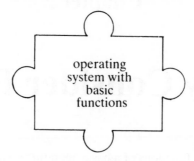

Figure 2.1

Suppose the proud owner of the new Itsy Bitsy 2000 with its operating
system now wants to extend his computer to do word processing. This is no
easy task. A list of possible packages has to be made, brochures obtained
and read, salesmen need to be consulted and an evaluation of the different
packages needs to be completed to find out which particular piece best fits
the operating system that is running on his machine. There may well be a
choice of ten different word processors or jigsaw pieces:

Type-sure
Letter Fast
Tripe Writer
Auto Type
Word Help
Letter Press
Mail Friend
Post Haste
Super Sec
Media Mate

A dealer will normally stock just two or three of these packages, perhaps
those which he considers to be the best, (or perhaps those with the highest
mark up!)

Figure 2.2

The three word processing packages shown in figure 2.2 on the short-list are Letter Fast, Word Help and Post Haste, each of which is a possible fit for the jigsaw. Each package is a different shape, has slightly different functions which work in slightly different ways, but will fit onto the basic operating system supplied with the computer. Each package will use and react to the operating system in a different way, and will be attached to the operating system differently. Each word processor may well hold the letters in a different format, which means that by attaching one of these packages the computer system becomes nonstandard.

Each word processor has a different way of producing a letter by using slightly different commands and symbols with assorted meanings, in the same way that operating systems differ. If a company has purchased two machines with a standard operating system, such as MS-DOS, it would expect the two systems to be totally compatible. In our example one computer system may be based in the Birmingham office and one in the London office, each location having the power to purchase its own added extras. The London secretary has worked with Post Haste before and so recommends that particular package. Meanwhile in Birmingham the salesman sells the most expensive, and of course best, word processor Letter Fast to the company. Both offices have word processing capabilities, but the two machines are now incompatible. The London office cannot send a floppy disk to Birmingham instead of a 500 page printed document because "Letter Fast" can not understand the way that "Post Haste" has saved the documents on the disk.

Pick and Integration

Many data processing managers frequently assume that they must adopt this patchwork of incompatible solutions in order to meet apparently different information and processing needs within an organisation. This fragmentation will inevitably lead to high cost, inflexible systems which, not surprisingly, fail to communicate with each other physically or logically.

The Pick system offers the computer manager a way out of the above maelstrom by serving a variety of end-user needs, from the efficient processing of transactions to the provision of information. A single integrated system can and is offered for both the information and the production centres of a business. Pick is done an injustice by being called just an operating system. It is much much more. It is an entire business system, a complete jigsaw with a standard picture, seen in figure 2.3.

The system still does all the functions a basic operating system should, communicating between man and machine. The extra facilities of Pick are integrated to form an operating system giving a sleek efficiency which is almost unobtainable with the cumbersome expensive add-on type of computer system . Due to this 'complete picture' concept Pick has the ability

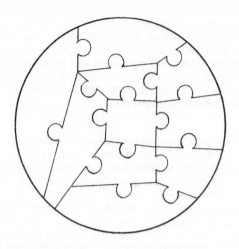

Figure 2.3 The complete jigsaw.

to apply to a particular set of business requirements. Information needs differ from company to company, person to person and often from moment to moment, and a computer system must be able to cater for all these needs. All computer systems, until Pick, were based on the assumption that organisations functioned on a fixed pattern, or at least could be forced to behave in a fixed way. Change was a nuisance, and if it did occur, a great deal of time and expense would result because the specified procedures on which the computer programs depended had been upset. Any business computer system should have the ability to enhance the processing of large amounts of available data, in order to derive the necessary information to assist with the control and operation of the business. Having up to date information available promptly, with the minimum of fuss, is of prime importance in today's business environment, where a computer should help rather than hinder. Even if only one or two key items are required, the effort often needed in extracting them from the total amount of information in a traditional operating system is both time consuming and expensive.

As technology proliferates and users become more demanding in their expectations and requirements, data processing managers are becoming increasingly concerned about the quality of the environment they are providing for their users. New, and in many cases untried, state-of-the-art systems are being bolted onto other new systems or onto the existing computing facilities. Problems are not only created by the actual hardware system, but the data administrator has to cope with the users and their perception of computing and what they would like it to achieve for them. Often personnel involved in the use of machines for the first time only have a short-sighted immediate view of what it can do. Varying requests from the users come at a later date when the knowledge of the system and it's abilities has built up.

As a result, end-users are faced with a number of incompatible software and hardware components. Physical incompatibilities lead inevitably to logical ones: data becomes fragmented; application systems fail to communicate properly with each other; the information coming out of the system is often not the anticipated result from the data going in! An ever increasing outlay on expensive technicians and application development staff sometimes manages to keep the edifice from crumbling, though from the end user's point of view it never appears as the single harmonious entity it was designed to be.

The problem put in simple terms is that the manager very often does not have the time to sort out the fundamentals of departmental problems. If he could provide a more flexible, efficient and cost-effective service, he would begin to convince the management that data processing could do more for the organisation. On another level, a major problem faced by all installations today is the ever widening gap between computer people and the actual users. Temporary solutions such as the personal computer and the information centre have been introduced, and found to be effective in the short term. In the longer term, unless great care is taken (and in the real world it rarely can be), the old incompatibilities and inflexibilities will resurface with renewed vigour. Proliferation of product types, the splitting of databases onto separate machines running in different environments; and the split in the company's staffing and orientation will come as variations on the old theme of high cost ineffective, inflexible systems. To the poor old end-user, who seems to be the industry scapegoat, the fragmentation not only seems unnecessary, but confusing and irritating as well.

One of the most important requirements for successful data processing is integration. The end-user should have one elementary system to deal with, both in terms of its appearance and also in terms of its implications. Sometimes an attempt is made to "bolt" different systems together and make them all look alike, by applying interfaces between the machines and the users. This approach only meets a small proportion of the objectives of integration, as the user will eventually see or be affected by the high costs and inflexibilities inherent in fragmentation and incompatibility.

If the computer manager, wanting an integrated easy-to-use system, scans the market place for systems with integration, he is generally going to be very disappointed. The typical traditional computing configurations do not come anywhere near meeting the company's need. Its complex, layered software is a crippling drawback, which means that a large machine, probably a mainframe, is needed to run all those layers.

If minicomputer architecture is considered for a data processing solution, some improvements may be seen. At first glance, the traditional minicomputer offers far lower acquisition and running costs, a more interactive orientation, and it covers the small to medium sized company profile more adequately than the mainframe does. Upon a more detailed investigation the minicomputer loses much of its charm. Commercial software is generally several years behind that available on the bigger machines; many of the native hardware suppliers are commercially unaware, and support can be poor to nonexistent.

Integration Achieved

The one system in today's market that will meet the need for integration is Pick. The Pick system is integrated in several dimensions, each of which is critical to the success of data processing within an organisation. Pick will run on machines of varying sizes. It will run compatibly on hardware from different manufacturers. It presents only *one* interface to the end user, whether he is interested in transaction processing or in the retrieval of information. The architecture is integrated within itself, incorporating operating system, database and enquiry language all as one unit.

By having an integrated solution the company in question effectively has extra human resources: those that otherwise would have been engaged in the continued maintenance, tuning and diagnosis involved in keeping a technically over-elaborate solution on its feet.

The Pick operating system has been available on various minicomputers for over ten years. The system has migrated up into mainframes and is now also available on many 16 bit micros. This mature product has most of the needed features for the new super micros but, having migrated from the larger systems, they show a potential for providing a new generic set of standards for creating a level of compatibility that has never before been possible.

In addition to the above advantages, Pick offers a low acquisition cost for a given level of application throughput (because of the low software overheads inherent in Pick, plus the fact that many implementations are partly in firmware). The low machine resource overheads associated with Pick can also be thought of as releasing large amounts of extra capacity. This extra capacity can be used for further application development, or for additional functions within the overall machine budget (say, for time and motion studies or for statistical analysis).

Pick offers a flexible, easy-to-use, remarkably powerful system that provides each and every user with total access to vital business data, giving full control of administrative functions. The staff employed do not need to be capable of programming, nor even have any previous experience of programming, to put the full capabilities of Pick to work. Often when looking for information on a particular subject it is not immediately obvious what information is required, yet it can be recognised when it is seen. Pick will allow the store of data to be browsed through and the selection of any items of particular interest. When you decide what you want, and the has been selected, it can be displayed in many ways including:

> Tabular summaries
> Comparisons
> Additional calculations
> Sorted lists

Pick contains all these facilities, allowing the user to reduce output to the information required, not hundreds of pages of print-out which tend to end up in the bin rather than being of any real use. The user decides on the format: tabular, on preprinted stationery, the entire report in UPPER CASE, or even in lower case. Once a report has been defined it can be saved for future re-use. This means the same report can be produced next month, or changes can be simply and easily applied. Pick gives managers (even those with no prior computing experience) the ability to answer questions quickly and simply, without the constraints of designing reports or sifting through a ream of print-out, thus giving access to information in a simple yet flexible manner.

Pick, being a fully integrated system allows applications software to be developed in the shortest possible time, requiring a minimum level of computer expertise.

In short, business people want solutions - not problems. They want easy, smooth information storage, retrieval and processing systems that anyone can use. They do not want complex components of a system that only an expensive systems analyst and senior programmer can operate, control and maintain.

Pick also solves the novice user's greatest headache. What exactly does he want from the computer system? Faced with the systems analyst, historically the new user has been pinned to the wall and been asked to specify, in absolute detail, precisely what the system should provide. Most people have a fairly clear idea of what they want the computer to achieve in broad outline, but what about all the small details ? Until someone has used the system they will not be aware of what small but important features can be incorporated in their software, or of what the machine is actually capable. How often has a system been set up, and mysteriously pages of enhancements appear! Pick allows the new user to start with a basic system which he is reasonably sure of and build upon it step by step, without incurring the penalties of redesigning a system. This is a way of evolving a finished system, based on experience of its operation. All these things are cost saving and give an efficient use of time.

Pick gives a business the ability to promote computing facilities within a company by increasing effectiveness. The user who selects Pick will suddenly find himself with more human and machine resources than he anticipated, and will be able to deliver better quality solutions more quickly than otherwise expected. While no-one is (as yet) claiming that Pick is perfect in all areas, it should be clear that Pick represents a sound foundation from which to build. The core of Pick is compatible with the developments and enhancements which take place on the basic system. Overall, it represents probably the lowest risk proposition available to a business today, and it is capable of a wide range of usage (which is covered in a later chapter.)

In the following chapters we shall be looking at how Pick achieves these claims, by looking at each piece of the Pick system jigsaw in turn.

Chapter 3

Databases

"Knowledge is of two kinds; we know a subject ourselves, or we know where we can find information upon it."

Dr Johnson

As anyone with a cluttered office knows, having large quantities of information on hand does not guarantee ready access to any particular piece of information.

Manual record keeping systems are limited and frequently cumbersome. They can be organised in only one way, for example according to subject in alphabetical order. Electronic files can be organised and used in several ways, quickly and accurately. Perhaps most importantly, electronic filing allows you to do more planning, book-keeping and evaluating of your business.

In Pick, the database is at the heart of the operating system giving the ability to handle information and make it available to anyone using the computer.

In this chapter we delve into database concepts with specific reference to Pick, and explain in some detail the underlying software architecture. This will allow us to discover certain issues which appear in database design and implementation, and will explain Pick's power in dealing with these issues.

What is a Database?

A database is, in essence, an organised, integrated collection of data. It is also rather more than this, since a collection of data has no particular value unless something can be done with it. The types of operation that one may wish to carry out on a database include:

> To access or retrieve particular data items from it.

> To search for a particular data item or, more importantly, a combination of data items.

To sort data items into a special order.

To update the information in it.

In this way, a database is a collection of data that is organised and integrated in such a way that the items can be retrieved or processed in any way that the user of the database may require, giving more control over the available data. The database structure allows the arrangement, combination and retrieval of data in a wide variety of ways. The information that is extracted can be displayed on a screen, changed or edited at a later date, integrated into an accounting suite of programs or even sent over a telephone line to another computer.

Data, Database and Information

A database is organised by ensuring that each item of data is stored in a structured coherent way, which in turn takes advantage of its relationships with other items of data in the database. In this way, an item can be accessed in any natural way by specifying its relationships to other items.

This is one of the major objectives of a database: to provide the means of sharing and relating data. Relationships between the various pieces of data are as important as the pieces of data themselves. It is important to note that a database stores data and not information. Information is derived from the facts and figures of the data. Data consists of isolated facts; a data item for example, may be "23". It is only when the information is processed in some way or associated with other data item in a meaningful context, that information is obtained.

A database must also be flexible enough to provide tomorrow's information needs as well as today's. How often has a database system been meticulously designed and implemented only to find that a new National Insurance law has been added to the many existing ones , resulting in a complete restructuring of the database? This in turn means alteration of any programs using those particular parts of the data base. *Access flexibility* is the ability to be able to access data easily and efficiently in a seemingly endless variety of ways. It means that the data base needs to be capable of dealing with unanticipated requirements which are usually provided for in the form of a query language.

Such a system can be invaluable to the business executive dealing in a dynamic and highly competitive environment. A database is integrated not only by ensuring that the same system is constantly applied to the storage of all items, but also avoids the duplication of data. This in turn maintains the database's integrity.

A program to create a database as well as providing the means for its interrogation is usually known as a Data Base Management System, (often shortened to DBMS).

Types of Database

There are two fundamental types of database known as *formatted* and *relational*.

Formatted or hierarchical databases

In a formatted database every entry has the same fixed format. The most common type of formatted system is the hierarchical database which is given its name because of the way data is organised. In each group of data, one attribute is designated as the master field and the other attributes are subordinate to it. Groups of the data are arranged in a manner similar to the rungs of a ladder and data can be retrieved only by traversing the levels according to the path defined by the master attributes. In Figure 3.1 there are four levels represented by the letters A to D. Hierarchical databases have been employed since the beginning of the modern period of computing, and require that the user's view of the data must be forced into a tree-like representation, again seen in Figure 3.1.

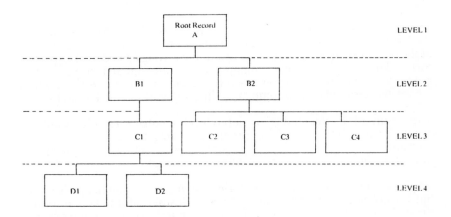

Figure 3.1 Hierarchy of files

The hierarchical database consists of a number of tables that must be scanned in a predetermined order to retrieve the required information. Figure 3.2 shows the steps that might be taken to find the list of Mozart's classical music in a record collection. The first table identifies the general category of the record in question. This can then be used to retrieve the table on the next level, which lists the composers or artists contained in the particular category. In turn this level can be used to retrieve information from the third level, about actual names of Mozart's classical works in the collection.

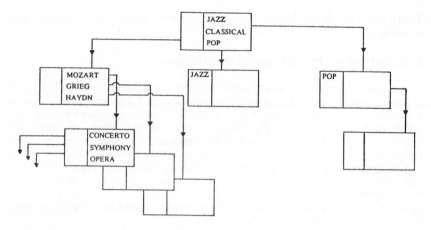

Figure 3.2 Searching for Mozart's Music

This type of system has the disadvantage that it is difficult to maintain, and the structure becomes very complex, forcing the user to formalise his view of the data in an artificial way. As a result, the setting up and working of this sort of database also becomes complex. As the amount and variety of data grows, so the hierarchy grows which often results in two pieces of data which are related residing on two completely different paths in the hierarchy.

The result of implementing a hierarchical database usually results in expensive and time consuming programs having to be written to keep relevant data together. This is an important point, as it explains the inflexibility inherent in hierarchical database design.

These systems can offer a high performance in certain limited applications, but do not satisfy the requirements for a flexible information resource. Prestel is a well known hierarchical database, but is a good demonstration of the inherent weakness of such a system.

Relational databases

On the other hand, Pick's objective is to be an information resource which is flexible and easy to use. This is based on the relational database model. The relational database is modelled upon the mathematical theory of relations, and was first developed by E. F. Codd of International Business Machines (IBM) in about 1970. This relatively new type of database concept is the subject of much interest as for the first time in computing it provides greater flexibility than other approaches.

In the Pick database, flexibility has been achieved by abolishing the hierarchy of levels - allowing any item of data to be used as a gateway to further information. All the data is stored in a two dimensional table, a row of which will contain all the information on, for example, an entry in a record collection.

TYPE	COMPOSER	TITLE
CLASSICAL	MOZART	CLARINET CONCERTO
CLASSICAL	GRIEG	PEER GYNT
POP	TEARS FOR FEARS	THE HURTING
CLASSICAL	MOZART	MAGIC FLUTE

Figure 3.3 Two dimensional record collection.

A relational database represents the user's view of the data. Relational databases also represent data as flat tables with the columns known as attributes and the rows (records) as tuples.

Databases are, by their very nature, large, so in reality vast tables are required. Each entry in the table is made up of a list of connected items; any subset of the items in the full list can be readily retrieved. No two rows of a table are identical but each has the ability to be uniquely identified, in our case by name and staff number. The rows or columns can be ordered in any manner, providing all the elements within the column are of the same type. The relational approach is based upon the principle that the relations between the data elements are the object of concern when retrieving information.

The rationalising of databases is effective and results in normalisation. For a database to be normalised there are four requirements:

Each table contains only one record type.

All rows are distinct - no duplication is allowed.

No data items may be empty.

The sequence of rows and columns is immaterial.

In a relational database each data item needs:

A name.

A definition.

A representative value.

A set of allowed values.

This data description is not held in the actual database but usually in a dictionary. The actual database contains occurrences of data, grouped into records, and associations between these occurrences. The associations are made using relational algebra and calculus.

Relational algebra

A relational operator takes one or more relations as its operands and from them produces a relation. A relationship implies an association between the attributes. There are no pointers to build and maintain, as there are in hierarchical databases, nor are there sets of processing relationships. Rather the data is modelled in a natural form of relations.

All operations on relations result in new relations. Thus a sequence of one or more operations on one or several relations gives a collection or tuples, with attribute domains. If the result has duplicate tuples, all but one of them is deleted as duplicates are not allowed in the definition of a relation.

Relational calculus

Relational calculus is another way to logically represent database operations. Like relational algebra, it neither depends on any particular physical data structure nor requires artificial constructs such as logical operators or sets. Unlike relational algebra, relational calculus is non-procedural. The algebraic approach isolates data items by applying operations on relations until only the desired items are left. The calculus approach isolates data items by name or by relationships to other items.

Relational models differ in several aspects from hierarchical models. For one, the relational model is based on a foundation of theory from relational mathematics. Another difference is that the relational model is more abstract. Hierarchical databases are directed at programming systems; the step from these to a programming language is a short one. The relational model consists of a group of concepts that are not particularly related to any programming language.

The relational model represents data as it exists and does not force the use of artificial constructs, rather it reduces data relationships to simpler components and then represents the components directly.

Using the relational model, Pick can handle many differing types of request for information simply by examining the rows and columns of data. It is this design of database which gives Pick its flexible, easy-to-use and remarkably powerful system. In other systems the otherwise independent data can now be associated with other elements in the database so that each user can access and retrieve information which is relevant to him and no one else , and not just in a format that has been predetermined by a systems designer.

Unlike the hierarchical model the internal structure and the user's view of the data are very similar which makes the conceptual jump between the data in the real world and the data in the computer much less difficult for the average user to comprehend.

Hashing a Database

The task of selecting one element from a file made up of many related records relies on the database management system being able to retrieve the element quickly and efficiently. There are several techniques available for arranging and facilitating the retrieval process, but the one used by Pick is called hashing.

Hashing involves performing an arithmetic operation on a field in the record using the result as an address for the data. As every house in the county has an unique address, so every line in the relational two dimensional table will have an unique address, except that it will be numerical rather than alphabetical.

An example of hashing is to take a simple arithmetic operation such as adding together the digits of the key to give the location.

Staff number	Department	Pay Scale
903	1	2
187	5	6
743	0	3
822	8	4
771	0	6
124	5	2
555	0	0
010	6	1
001	8	5
233	9	2
421	0	1
541	0	4

This is the original file in the two dimensional format. Adding together the digits of the staff number will give us the actual storage address of that particular line in the hashed file.

For example: Staff Number 903 = (9+0+3) = 12th position in hashing table.

	Staff Number	Department	Pay Scale
01	010	6	1
02	001	8	5
03			
04			
05			
06			
07	124	5	2
08	233	9	2
09	421	0	1
10	541	0	4
11			
12	903	1	2
13	822	8	4
14	743	0	3
15	771	0	6
16	187	5	6
17	553	0	0

The hashing takes place by taking one line at a time from the original table and calculating its address. In the case of item 010 the addition of all the digits come to 1, so the record is placed in position 1. The next entry in the original table is 001, which when summed is also equal to 1, but the slot 01 is already filled so it goes to the next available spare slot, in this case 02.

This technique means that only selected lines in a file need to be scanned. In other types of retrieval process every line in a file is scanned separately, resulting in a search of a file with 10,000 items taking 100 times longer than for a file containing 100 items.

The latter type of searching is like going to a library to find a book and starting the search at the bookcase nearest the door and examining each book until the one wanted is found! The hashing routine makes sure you get to the book you are looking for directly, for the book number gives the bookcase, shelf and the position on that shelf, very much like a grid reference.

The Query Language

A database management system should also provide the ability to obtain information from a database on an *ad hoc* basis. This is achieved using an interactive "query" language. This is one of the most important parts of the system as it makes the database both accessible and useful. The query language in Pick gives the ability to:

Handle spontaneous information retrieval.

Provide a convenient English-type and non-programmer-oriented means of using the system.

Enable the access of parts of the database which satisfy a set of data content qualifications.

The query language (Access) has commands which are self-standing. That is they are unrelated and processed individually by the database system. The query language gives the ability to access data on the basis of any nominated point as well as being able to browse through the data. The flexibility of this query language is far beyond the limited accessing facilities provided by programming languages using file access methods adopted on conventional operating systems.

Database query languages can be divided into two major groups: procedural and non-procedural. A procedural query language is one in which a list of instructions is supplied to the computer in the form of a 'procedure' which the user must supply before the problem can be solved. A non-procedural language allows the user to request the answer without telling the computer how to obtain that answer.

A powerful non-procedural language such as Pick's Access can be used by the absolute computer novice, as no understanding of the database structure is required. An information request about members of staff might be:

    LIST STAFF WITH CHILDREN

The results might be displayed as:

STAFF NUMBER	CHILD
010	ALASTAIR
001	LUCY
612	CHARLES

As we have seen, database access is a two-step process. Firstly the required data must be found and secondly it must be displayed in a relevant format.

Finding this information may be difficult if the request involves several data relationships and if the database structure is complex. Also, the user may have several ways to request the data. To the user they are equivalent but, to the database system, one way may result in easy access and efficient processing, while the other may be slow and cause repetitive, wasteful, to-and-fro-processing.

Once the data is found, it must be presented to the user in a familiar and useful format. For example if the retrieval process produces a 10,000 item list, most users would just leave it sitting on their desk and ultimately file it in the bin! Information, such as averages and totals would probably be far more useful and meaningful than the entire list being printed.

Such problems of database access are usually handled by the system without the user being aware of any potential problem. You should be aware of these functions, however, as we will discuss these topics in later chapters.

Pick Database Processing - The Advantages

Once using Pick, any operational information that an organisation has stored on the database is in one standard and coherent format. Once this standardisation has taken place, all data is available making it accessible and therefore valuable as an information asset. By replacing a series of files with a fully integrated database the task of relating all the different pieces of data becomes much easier and less prone to error.

The time needed to develop new systems or to respond to bespoke requests is drastically reduced. Bespoke enquiries can be performed by anyone, not just the company "computer expert" or the "overpaid programmer". The result of using a database allows information to be obtained from existing data quickly and efficiently.

Data integrity

Another important advantage of relational databases is the elimination of data duplication. If data is recorded in two places on a system then the database will lack integrity. Integrity refers to a variety of tasks in the database environment, the main ones being :

> The co-ordination of data accessing by different applications.

> Policing the propagation of information being updated.

> The preservation of a high degree of consistency and correctness of data.

With many different users sharing various portions of the database, it is impossible for each individual user to be responsible for the consistency of the information. The database maintains the relationships of the user's data items to all other data items, some of which may be unknown to the user or prohibited for the user to access.

If data is recorded in two places it is easy for one value to be changed and the other not. The separate data items then disagree with each other and may be retrieved by two people, resulting in two reports that conflict; this soon leads to a general mistrust of the computer's ability. One of the major objectives of the Pick database is to maintain control and preserve the integrity of the database.

Database processing can lead to better data management within an organisation. When data is centralised in one place, keeping up with and maintaining that information is easier.

By using the Pick database, any software programs such as stock control or accounting will interface directly with the files. This means that any changes in the files need to be accommodated by the software programs, and vice versa. The Pick database will allow changes in either area with the minimum of fuss and bother. With many other systems it can take weeks to change a piece of software or the structure of the data. In Pick the data and the program are independent of each other rather than being intricately tied to each other, allowing easy maintenance for any given system.

The Need for Record Locking

When using a database, which is being shared with other users, two or more users may want to retrieve the same data concurrently. This poses many problems. Consider what would happen to the database if the following sequence of events were to happen.

1. Fred retrieves staff record 010 from the database.

2. Jim retrieves staff record 010, not the real thing but just another copy.

3. Fred changes the record and replaces it in the database.

4. Jim changes the record and replaces it in the database.

The changes that Fred made will have been overwritten by Jim's amended record, so Fred's changes have disappeared. To avoid this happening, the Pick operating system has a series of levels at which a *lock out* of a user can occur. The record is locked against being retrieved until it has been placed back. But, this lock out system can lead to other problems. Let us say that Fred exclusively locks staff record 101 and Jim locks staff record 102. Next, Fred tries to lock record 102. Since record 102 has already been locked by Jim the system will not give control to Fred, instead it puts Fred on a waiting list for the record when Jim has finished with it. Now suppose Jim tries to lock record 101. It is already locked by Fred, so the system puts Jim onto a waiting list for 101. The result is Jim is waiting for Fred, and Fred is waiting for Jim. The two users will never finish the tasks. The Pick Database Management System monitors the users for a declaration of intent to modify or delete a record, preventing this type of locking from ever occurring.

Summary

The advantages of Pick relational processing include: more timely information; more information; less data duplication; program and data independence; better data management and economies of scale.

The Pick integral relational database management, and English-like query capability, allows several users to concurrently access a common database and format their own reports without having to develop unique programs. For example, since all users may share the same data base, an authorised person in accounting can easily obtain up-to-date reports from marketing by using simple interactive statements. Moreover, the relational database manager provides the capability to interactively analyse data and dynamically manipulate and manage files. As an integral part of the operating system, its feature include:

1. Sharing of data among multiple users and departments, eliminating data access barriers that can occur in systems where each department has its own files.

2. Data is recorded only once, by the department that controls it, without the need for duplication in other departments who may need to retrieve the information.

3. Data files on the database may have the relationships between the items of data changed or added without any impact upon existing data files.

4. An easy to use query language which is relatively free-form, giving automatic or user specified output report formats in either columnar or non-columnar forms. The query language also provides generalised data selection using logical and arithmetic selection criteria.

Chapter 4

Files and Structures

The term 'file', as used in the context of the Pick operating system, refers to the mechanism for maintaining a set of like items logically together. Files are organised in a hierarchical structure, with files at one level pointing to multiple files at a lower level. Four distinct file levels exist and this chapter explains the purpose and structure of level 4.

The Nature of a File and its Structure

A file is an organised collection of related information, and any computer system is comprised of files of information. In that respect the computer has become an electronic filing cabinet.

In the Pick operating system all information, including the language for data retrieval, is held in the same type and structure of files. Other operating systems work with many different types of files, both in concept and structure, leading to a complex and confusing lifestyle. The structure and workings of the Pick files are central to the operation of the operating system. As in a "paper" file, a computer file is a way of keeping similar information together in one place. For instance, one file may contain the census returns for all the people in one village or county. Files can be organised in different ways. Pick files are arranged in a hierarchical manner with four distinct levels, shown in Figure 4.1.

In Figure 4.1 it can be seen that files at one level point to multiple files at a lower level. At each level an 'existence' check takes place. For instance, the system dictionary will check for the presence of user A's master dictionary, before allowing the level to be traversed, and so on all the way down the chain. An example is shown in Figure 4.2. When user A is working on the stock files and then wishes to view the sales ledger, the path is reversed and a new path started down the user B path from the system dictionary.

At first glance this seems like the diagrams and explanations about the hierarchical database discussed in the last chapter, but there is one important difference. The database consists of the lowest level of the files, i.e. all the data files. It is these data files which are related together to form the database facility.

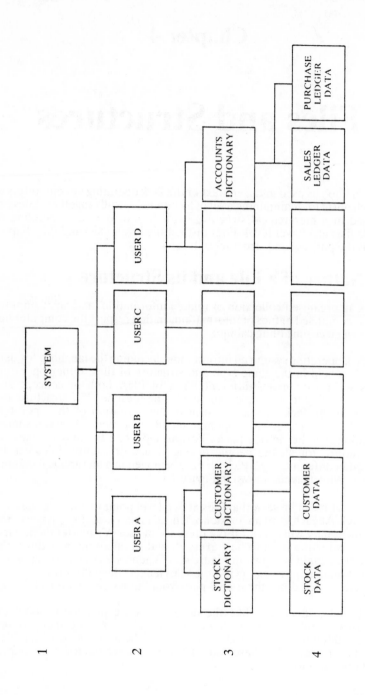

Figure 4.1 The levels of files

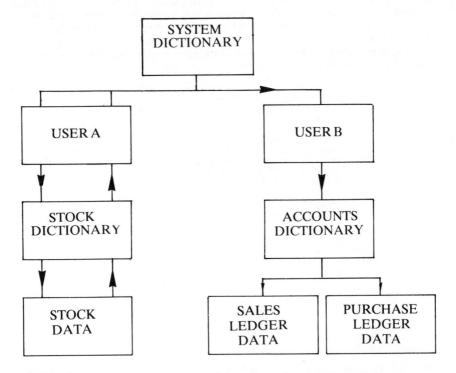

Figure 4.2

Each of these four levels of files has a specific task and purpose within the Pick operating system. In the rest of this book these tasks and the structure of each of the file levels will be explained individually. We now start with the lowest level, the data files.

Data Files

The process of handling a great many pieces of paper is common in any business. It is these pieces of paper which contain information and data about the organisation; the muddle that they get into sometimes seems almost inevitable. For this reason, offices have developed various methods for keeping all the paper in an orderly and retrievable state. Like "paper" files, data stored on a computer file needs to be organised to enable it to be of some use in the future. Items need to be organised in such a way as to facilitate retrieval; there is little point in filing something if it cannot be located again.

If we view a computer as an electronic filing cabinet, then the operating system is acting as a secretary. A file is not unlike a complete card index containing, for instance, a card for every customer. Usually the cards are filed in some semblance of order, quite often alphabetically. In Figure 4.3 the cards are filed by customer name. In other words, the customer name is the criterion by which the card index is referenced.

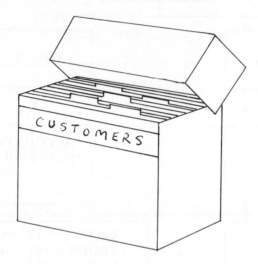

Figure 4.3 A traditional card box

An item in such a file is one card containing all known information about a customer. A computer file will have facilities for the nominated customer name or keyword to be used as the reference point for searching, enabling one item to be distinguished or picked out from all the other items in that file.

If, in the card file, we wish to find out what items the brewery supplies to the Green Man pub, the procedure would be as follows: Locate the card-box, go through the file index to "G". Having found the section for "G" then individually look at every card until the one headed Green Man is found. The word Green Man is the reference point that is used for the search mechanism. With this type of file (which is very common in computing), the only way to find the information on the Green Man pub is by searching specifically for the customer name.

Pick files are not restricted to using just the customer name. If this card file was put onto a Pick system number of keywords could be used. The three cards that are shown in Figure 4.4 might also be selected by using the word 'tonic' as a selection criterion enabling all the pubs with tonic on the "supply" line to be selected. This eliminates the need for looking at each card sequentially and individually.

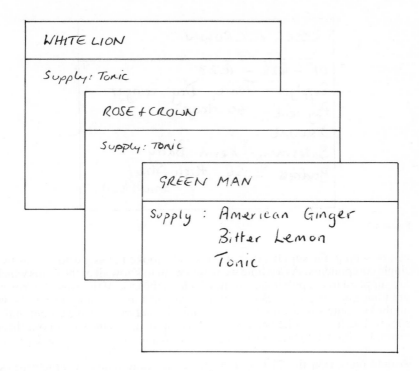

Figure 4.4 Three individual cards

Record attributes

In a card index there is only so much room on a piece of card for putting information. Likewise each item stored on a Pick machine has a maximum size of 32K of data (32,267 characters). Items can be divided into fields called attributes, and there may be as many of these as is wished within an item.

In Figure 4.5 showing the record of the Rose & Crown pub there are six attributes or pieces of information apart from the name of the Pub contained on the card. They are the phone number, the items supplied to the pub, payment terms, amount of discount allowed off list price, the salesman responsible for the pub, and the address of the establishment in question.

In any file there will be multiple elements or components of this kind that can be referred to as a single entity. If the yearly calendar was stored as a file, it must be possible to refer to a single date as well as being able to refer to a month or the entire year. In the above card this type of elemental structuring

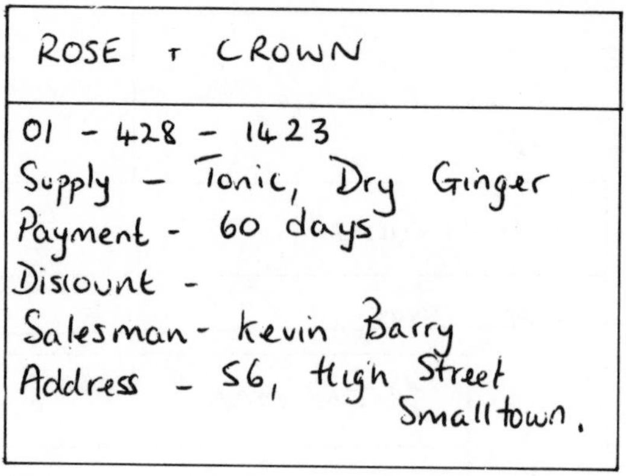

```
ROSE & CROWN

01 - 428 - 1423
Supply - Tonic, Dry Ginger
Payment - 60 days
Discount -
Salesman - Kevin Barry
Address - 56, High Street
                    Smalltown.
```

Figure 4.5

can be seen in the supply attribute. It can be looked at as a whole or as two single components. As a whole we would want to know all of the items which are supplied to the pub in question, which, in the case of the Rose & Crown, are tonic and dry ginger. But in another circumstance we may wish to know all the customers to whom we supply tonic; in that case, each element of the supply data has to looked at as separate component. In the case of our three examples this would bring up the customers White Lion and Rose & Crown.

A data record on the Pick system possesses some unique characteristics. These in turn form a very powerful data structure of which the operating system takes full advantage.

The attributes in an item are numbered starting from zero; attribute zero contains the item identifier which is unique to that item. This attribute is the only one with any restrictions and rules for usage. Attribute zero will always be treated by the operating system as the key word, and that key word can be no more than 50 characters long.

The data that follows the item identifier (often abbreviated to item-id), is divided into more attributes. Each attribute can contain one or more values, with each of those values being separated by a special marker. An attribute containing more than one value is termed multi-valued. Each value of a multi-valued attribute can contain multiple subvalues, also separated by special markers and termed subvalue attributes. Attributes, values and subvalues are individually variable in length and can grow and shrink as required, occupying only as much disk storage as they require plus the special markers that separate them. If we look at Figure 4.6 showing the card for the White Lion, it can be seen that the supply information consists of several parts. The supply line would be an attribute, and each item supplied would be a multi-value.

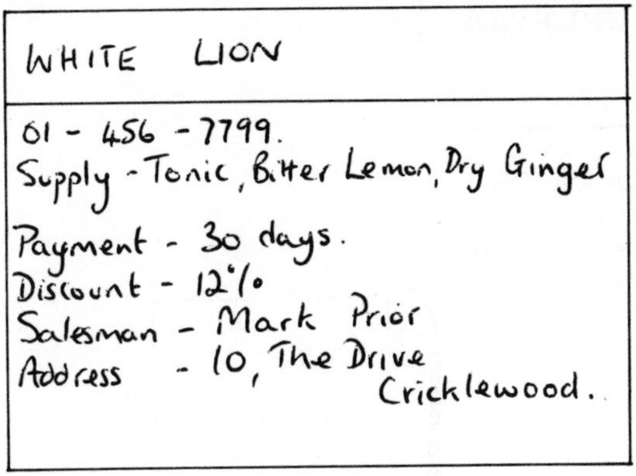

```
WHITE   LION

01 - 456 - 7799.
Supply - Tonic, Bitter Lemon, Dry Ginger

Payment - 30 days.
Discount - 12%
Salesman - Mark Prior
Address  - 10, The Drive
                    Cricklewood.
```

Figure 4.6

For this particular customer sales file there is one item for each establishment that is supplied. For each item there are six attributes plus the key attribute zero, each attribute is held on a separate line in the file. Each attribute contains one of the pieces of information that is held on the card.

```
Attribute 0 WHITE LION
          1 01-456-7799
          2 TONIC]DRY GINGER]BITTER LEMON
          3 30
          4 12
          5 MARK PRIOR
          6 10 THE DRIVE CRICKLEWOOD
```

Any attribute may contain multiple values, and any multiple value can contain subvalues. In the above example, attribute 2 contains several products sold to the White Lion pub, so it is a multi-value. The attribute remains globally known as the supply attribute, which actually consists of three values separated by a special marker - "]". Graphically, the above example can be represented as seen in Figure 4.7

This type of record keeping is satisfactory as long as a history of the sales to a specific pub is not required. Every time the salesman for a particular pub leaves the company or moves to a different sales area a new card needs to be made out. The history of the White Lion can be seen in Figure 4.8. Each salesman has sold different products to the publican, in different quantities, with different discounts. The old cards, indicating the success or failure, of a salesman can easily become lost.

43

Attribute

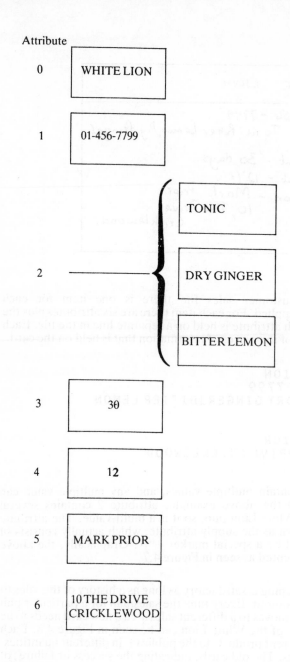

0   WHITE LION

1   01-456-7799

2   TONIC

        DRY GINGER

        BITTER LEMON

3   30

4   12

5   MARK PRIOR

6   10 THE DRIVE CRICKLEWOOD

Figure 4.7

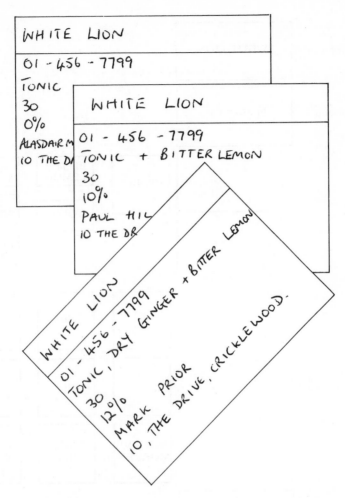

Figure 4.8 History of the White Lion

This sort of loss and fragmentation of information can be avoided by keeping all the past and present information on one computerised "record card" as graphically represented in Figure 4.9.

The salesmen for the White Lion pub were first Alasdair Morren, secondly Paul Hill and thirdly Mark Prior. Each salesman has achieved different product sales and different discount rates. In attribute 4 the first figure is the discount that Alasdair Morren was able to offer the publican, Paul Hill offered 10% and Mark Prior 12%. Attribute 2 shows that two of the salesmen have managed to sell more than one product, so the multi-value is split into sub values. This is seen in the file by the use of the character "\".

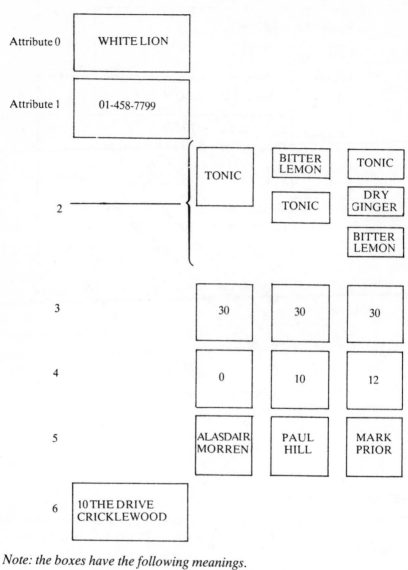

| Attribute 0 | WHITE LION |
| Attribute 1 | 01-458-7799 |

2

TONIC	BITTER LEMON	TONIC
	TONIC	DRY GINGER
		BITTER LEMON

3

| 30 | 30 | 30 |

4

| 0 | 10 | 12 |

5

| ALASDAIR MORREN | PAUL HILL | MARK PRIOR |

6

| 10 THE DRIVE CRICKLEWOOD |

Note: the boxes have the following meanings.

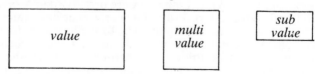

value   *multi value*   *sub value*

Figure 4.9

Where Alasdair Morren has only managed to sell one item it is represented by an ordinary multi-value. An attribute can contain as many multi-values as required up to a limit of 32,000 characters (which is the limit of a single attribute). A multi-value is as elastic as is required by the user, containing many multi-values or only a few. Multi-valued and sub-valued fields can be manipulated by all of the components of the operating system: Access, DATA/BASIC, PROCs and the Editor. (Each of which will be discussed later.) Essentially, multi-values and subvalues can be added, deleted, located or retrieved from any given field with great ease. When the data is displayed on a screen via the database query language Access, the attribute marks "]" are converted into carriage returns so the display is easy to read in the form of one line entries. When the actual stored data is displayed on the screen or printed it will be output as shown below:

```
0 WHITE LION
1 01-458-7799
2 TONIC]TONIC\BITTER LEMON]TONIC\DRY
GINGER\BITTER LEMON
3 30]30]30
4 0]10]12
5 ALASDAIR MORREN]PAUL HILL]MARK PRIOR
6 10 THE DRIVE CRICKLEWOOD
```

Notice that attribute 0, the item identifier, is not given a line number. Although it is an attribute, it has become reserved for its special purpose as a keyword. Because the location of the data on disk is dependent on the contents of attribute 0 it can not be altered and therefore is not given a line number. Later in the book it will be shown how entries in the file dictionary give special meaning to the line items for interpretation by the data retrieval facilities and how more useful print-outs than the above can be formatted.

In the above examples we have not been at all bothered by the length of the data. This is because the Pick file structure is dynamically variable. Although each new attribute is stored on a new line, only the characters on that line are held, none of the blank spaces are stored. Variable length files, records, and fields provide efficient storage utilisation. Since there are no fixed length fields, as in conventional computing, you only use as much space as is needed and never have to reserve extra space 'just in case' the file you are working on becomes bigger than anticipated. The traditional approach to attributes was to define them all in advance and to "fix" them at a certain length. That is to say each field has a predefined length and position within the item. This has the knock-on effect of the item itself being of a fixed and standard length. The salesmens' name attribute when held in a fixed length format should be at least 20 characters long to ensure that 99% (there's always an odd one out) of possible names can be entered; however this would involve the storing of unnecessary space characters.

With these salesmen's names there are 34 characters which make up the names (including the space character between the first and surname), leaving 26 redundant spaces that are stored on disk as actual data - what a waste of space. Only in the case of getting a name like Rowland Mecklenburgh, when all twenty allocated spaces are used would this type of fixed file be efficient. But should there be a name longer than 20 characters, such as Rowland's brother Jonathan, the last name will be come truncated and cut off in its prime.

J O N A T H A N   M E C K L E N B U R G

In Pick this does not happen due to the variable length fields. In the data files there are two types of variability: one in the length of the data attribute (and therefore the item), and the other in the number of items present in a file. In many commercial systems the size of the file is fixed, and to expand those fixed files is quite a daunting task which needs qualified, experienced personnel. In Pick the files grow with you, dynamically as required.

When only the salesman's name and no spaces are stored then the length is variable. In total, 34 characters are stored rather than 60. The variable length attributes eliminate all the wasted space that occurs in systems using fixed length files. The variable length file structure which is supported provides significant savings in terms of on-line disk space requirements, by increasing the efficient utilisation and disk access. This feature generates a flexible data structure which is hard to match.

Conclusion

These features make the system easy to use and easy to learn. Multi-values and subvalues generate a flexible data structure which is handled very easily by a computer novice.

So far, there are pieces of data in variable length format, collected together to give items, each with a unique identifier, in the data file. In the next level up in the file hierarchy is the data dictionary file which is used to describe the structure of the file(s) found below it. The existence of the data file and the associated data dictionary are linked. The data can only be accessed via a dictionary, and no single file can exist without a dictionary to define its location and structure. In addition to storing the location of a file on disk, the information contained in the file dictionary serves as a road map for retrieving data from the associated data file when using the retrieval language Access.

Chapter 5

Dictionary Files

Dictionary Files and Their Structure

The reporting functions achieved by the query language of the database are achieved by associating with each data file a dictionary file which contains coded information about each of the various data attributes and how they are to be displayed. In a relational database each date item needs at least:

>A name.
>A definition.

and, optionally:

>A representative value.
>A range of allowed values.

It is important to remember that a file dictionary has the same structure as any other file held on the Pick system; every file consists of a number of items, each referenced by a item identifier and consisting of any number of attributes.

So why a separate section on dictionaries, when the data file structure has already been explained? Well, dictionary files do have the same basic structure but with certain constraints. Each item in a dictionary file must be in a particular format in order for the system to perform data retrieval functions for which the Pick system is renowned. Every data file is found, at the fourth file level, as seen in the hierarchical diagram in the previous chapter. Directly above the data file level are the data dictionaries.

Although the detail explained in this chapter on dictionary files may seem at times somewhat tedious, it is important to understand the structure of them. Dictionary files are one of the cornerstones in understanding how Pick works and examples of dictionary items are used constantly in following chapters to illustrate features not yet discussed.

Every data file needs to be associated with a dictionary. In Figure 5.1 the customer dictionary is associated with two data files. The file dictionary con-

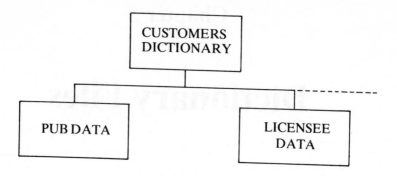

Figure 5.1

tains attributes which define the structure of the data and how that data is to be presented on the screen or on paper.

For instance, to find all the customers who are privileged to have Paul Hill as their salesman, the command:

LIST CUSTOMERS WITH SALESMAN "PAUL HILL"

needs to be entered. The word *customers* refers to the data file in which the relevant data is stored. The word *salesman* is a label, associated with a particular attribute of the named data file. In our example, attribute 5 of every customer card contains the salesman's name.

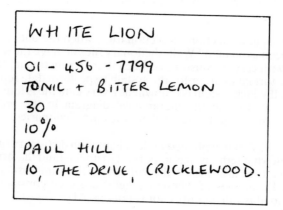

Figure 5.2

The label given is, in fact, the item identifier which the query language processor uses to fetch data. The example command above looks at every attribute 5 in the customer file, and then passes the items which have the value "PAUL HILL" residing in that attribute back to the Pick query language for output.

The item identifier (see previous chapter), of a dictionary item is the name which the data attribute is associated to and is to be called when using the query language. The provision of a dictionary item SALESMAN in the dictionary for the CUSTOMER file enables the query language to locate and output the data as every item in the dictionary file is associated to one particular attribute in every item in the data file. This is shown in Figure 5.3.

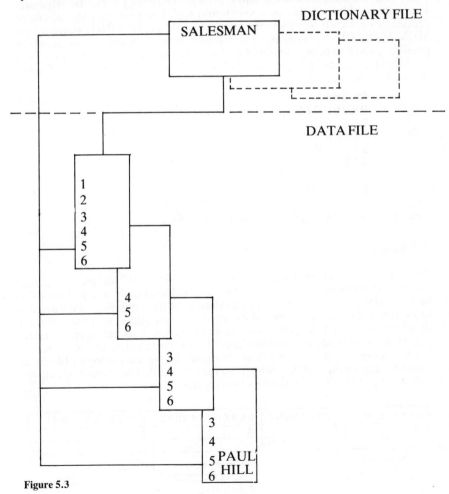

Figure 5.3

Data Dictionary Attributes Explained

The structure of the dictionary file is always the same, in that each is composed of a number of items, and each item is divided into attributes. In a dictionary, each attribute in an item has a specific purpose, which is briefly explained in the following paragraphs.

Attribute 0

This, as in the data files, is the name used for retrieving a specific attribute. It is best to think of this as a shorthand tag. For example, the attribute representing a club membership number could be MEMNO, standing for MEMBERSHIP NUMBER. The chosen name should be as short as possible as well as being meaningful. The entry for the item identifier is used by Access as an information retrieval word. For the pub's customer file the dictionary file might be:

```
PHONE
PRODUCTS
DISCOUNT
PAYMENT
SALESMAN
ADDRESS
PURCH.AMNT
DISCOUNT.AMNT
```

Each word describes an attribute in the data file.

Attribute 1

This can be one of two values "A" or "S". The "A" defines an actual attribute definition, i.e. that the data is in the file already and just needs to be located to be output. "S" indicates that some manipulation of data needs to be done. For instance, two data attributes are added together. Rather than store three pieces of information, store the two relevant figures, and let a dictionary item add the two together. This is particularly useful if the two figures being added are constantly changing. Using the customer file as an example, the amount of discount given may be needed as a figure, giving the following attributes in the data dictionary file.

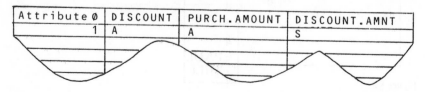

Attribute 0	DISCOUNT	PURCH.AMOUNT	DISCOUNT.AMNT
1	A	A	S

Attribute 2

This is the Attribute Mark Counter (AMC or field number of the data file). It keeps count of the number of fields that have been defined for a particular file. This attribute also gives information on the attribute position in the data file.

Att	0	DISCOUNT	PURCH.AMOUNT	DISCOUNT.AMNT	SALESMAN
	1	A	A	S	A
	2	7	4	99	5

Attribute 2 of item DISCOUNT has the value of 4 telling us that the discount information is to be found in attribute 4 of each item in the data file, just as SALESMAN is always found in attribute 5. Each dictionary item represents a column in the conceptual two dimensional table, giving the operating system the column in which to look for the information.

DISCOUNT.AMNT, does not point directly to a piece of data, so has a false AMC - in this case, 99. The AMC is greater than the number of attributes present in the data file, so no association to data is immediately made. The actual calculation of amount of discount is done in a later attribute.

This numbering of the data attributes should be unique. No other data element should occur at the same field position, unless deliberately. However, it is possible to use the same field position to create a synonym. This means that the same value can be accessed in part or in whole using different names. This can be useful when data has various aspects to various users in an organisation. On one person's document number could be another person's receipt identifier. It also allows data attributes to be accessed using more than one language. To make a synonym you simply define two fields in the same position, but with different item identifiers. If the same attribute is simply being renamed it is practical to keep all other characteristics the same; the two synonym items can be used to access the same data, or parts of the same data. For example, the dictionary item SALESMAN could also have a synonym REP, which would be associated with the same data.

Attribute	0	SALESMAN	REP
	1	A	A
	2	5	5

This allows a flexible vocabulary of terms to be built up.

Once the attribute position in the data file has been decided it should not be altered, this is because the field position is used by the system as a reference to the actual physical storage positions on disk.

Attribute 3

This may optionally contain the text which is to appear at the heading of the column for the defined data field when it is displayed using the query language. A multi-line heading can be specified by including all the desired characters in attribute 3, with the character "]" separating the lines.

Att	Ø	DISCOUNT	PURCH.AMOUNT	DISCOUNT.AMNT	SALESMAN
	1	A	A	S	A
	2	7	4	99	5
	3	DISCOUNT		DISCOUNT]AMNT	SALESMAN]NAME

The above contents of attribute 3 will be displayed as column headings when used via the Access language. The text in this attribute may be anything, and not necessarily the same as the item identifier. If no text is entered then the item identifier is automatically used as a column heading. The above table will be displayed as follows:

```
DISCOUNT   PURCH.AMOUNT   DISCOUNT   SALESMAN
                          AMNT       NAME
```

DISCOUNT.AMNT and SALESMAN are displayed on two lines. A new line is actioned by the "]" character.

Attribute 4

This attribute offers the facility to define a set of attributes that are controlled by a single attribute. The controlling attribute is known as the parent, and is used to indicate dependency by other attributes. For any potential value of the parent there are several potential values of the children. But, for one potential value of one of the children there is only one possible value of the parent.

For instance, if we examine a bank, each branch has a separate code to uniquely identify it. In the table below it has been called SORT.CODE. This is the parent attribute, for dependent upon this value are the branch account numbers. This relationship can be represented in attribute 4. SORT.CODE is controlling attribute 2 (ACNO) defined by C;2 and ACNO is dependent upon the value of SORT.CODE defined by D;1.

This attribute is rarely used in data dictionaries.

item-id		SORT.CODE	ACNO
attribute	001	A	A
	002	1	2
	003	SORT]CODE	ACCOUNT]NUMBER
	004	C;2	D;1

Attributes 5 and 6

These are not used in the data dictionary definitions, and must be null, not even containing any space characters. When creating a dictionary item with the editor, the user must be careful to create null lines (see editing techniques for further information).

The data dictionary items now look as follows:

Att 0	DISCOUNT	PURCH.AMOUNT	DISCOUNT.AMNT	SALESMAN
1	A	A	S	A
2	7	4	99	5
3	DISCOUNT		DISCOUNT]AMNT	SALESMAN]NAME
4				
5				
6				

Attributes 7 and 8

Attributes 7 and 8 include various types of code for the formatting of data for output purposes. One of these categories is conversion codes. Conversions are codes specified in dictionary definition which enable certain types of data values to be converted from one format to another. A common and most frequent use of this facility is for date and time to be converted. The date can take many forms, including:

> 15 MAY 1980
> 15/05/1980
> 15-05-80

The way dates are presented differ from person to person, so the Pick system stores dates in a standard form and allows conversion to the required form.

The form stored internally by the Pick system is a four figured number; each new day the number is increased by one. For instance, 1st March 1985 is represented by the number 6720, the 28th February would have been 6719 and the 2nd March 6721.

This date counting system used by Pick is both individual and different. The number appears somewhat arbitrary, but is in fact the number of days counted since 31 December 1967. This date appears a weird choice until one of the Pick legends is told. Richard Pick set the first Pick type operating system running on that date!

There are various date conversion codes available (for converting the internal number to a display format and a display format in an Access statement into an internal form):

LIST DELIVERIES WITH DATE "1 MAR 1985"

The first stage of processing this command is for the date to be converted from its external format (1 MAR 1985) to its internal format (6720). Each of the date records are then searched for the internal date (6720) When all those deliveries which are due at the factory on day 6720 have been found (i.e. the attribute DATE = 1234) the output is converted into external format for the report. This internal number system is not only more economical to store than the external dates, but makes the equality operations such as, "less than" and "greater than" much easier to process. For example:

LIST CUSTOMER WITH LAST.VISIT BEFORE "21 OCT 1985 "

This would list all the customers who were visited before 21st October 1985.

Information can become somewhat confusing when dealing with internal dates before the 31 Dec 1967, as the number held is negative.

The storage format for times is the number of seconds from midnight of any one day. A time value held in this form may be listed in the standard display format by including in the dictionary definition for that item the code MT in attribute 7. The standard display format for the time is hh:mm, where hh is the hour (in twenty four hour format) and the mm is the minutes past the hour.

There are various time conversions available, differing only in the displayed version which is specified by the user.

A further conversion code deals with numeric values. The storage medium for numbers, including those with decimal points, parts of numbers (fractions), and all the other types of numerical representation are applied by using an appropriate conversion code on attribute 7 of the dictionary definition

```
attribute  0      AGE        DATE.OF.BIRTH
```

001	S	A
002	99	2
003	AGE	DATE OF] BIRTH
004		
005		
006		
007		D2/

The conversion code D2/ outputs the date of birth data in the format 15/06/ 55, AGE has no need to be formatted as it is just a figure, say 32.

Attribute 9

This attribute must contain a valid definition code which indicates the required type of justification

        L Left justify
        R Right justify
        T Text justify
        U Unfold justify

Justification of fields defines how they will appear when displayed. It is customary for the numeric fields to be justified to the right so that they can be shown in columns

        99.99
        888.88

For letters (alphanumeric) it is usual to align to the left

        Tim Blower
        28 Dead End
        Croydon

```
attribute  0      AGE        DATE.OF.BIRTH
```

001	S	A
002	99	2
003	AGE	DATE OF] BIRTH
004		
005		
006		
007		D2/
008		
009	L	R

Attribute 10

This attribute must contain an integer which specifies the width of the column which will be allocated to the defined field on output. As explained earlier, this has absolutely no effect on the actual length of the value which may be held on the data file, but controls only the output format.

Attribute 0	AGE	DATE.OF.BIRTH
001	S	A
002	99	2
003	AGE	DATE OF] BIRTH
004		
005		
006		
007		D 2 /
008		
009	L	R
010	2	8

For the above date values the length is calculated by counting the characters plus the dividing slashes, in this case eight.

So if we were to look at the data for the pubs which were used as examples earlier we would have a two dimensional table looking something like Figure 5.4.

WHITE LION	01-458 7799	TONIC	30	0	ALASDAIR MORREN	10, THE DRIVE CRICKLEWOOD
WHITE LION	01-458 7799	BITTER LEMON	30	10	PAUL HILL	10, THE DRIVE CRICKLEWOOD
WHITE LION	01-458 7799	TONIC	30	10	PAUL HILL	10, THE DRIVE CRICKLEWOOD
WHITE LION	01-458 7799	TONIC	30	12	MARK PRIOR	10, THE DRIVE CRICKLEWOOD
WHITE LION	01-458 7799	DRY GINGER	30	12	MARK PRIOR	10, THE DRIVE CRICKLEWOOD
WHITE LION	01-458 7799	BITTER LEMON	30	12	MARK PRIOR	10, THE DRIVE CRICKLEWOOD

Figure 5.4 Pub data represented in a flat table. Each line in the table is unique, with no repetition of data. The table has no repetition of columns, so for each 'product supplied' a new line is necessary.

If this data is required for output the dictionary items may look something like Figure 5.5.

Item Identifier	NAME	PHONE	GOODS	PAYMENT	DISCOUNT	SALESMAN
Attribute 1	5	A	A	A	A	A
2	0	1	2	3	4	5
3	NAME	TELEPHONE	SUPPLY	PAYMENT]TERMS	DISCOUNT	SALESMAN
4						
5						
6						
7						
8						
9	L	L	L	R	R	T
10	20	13	15	3	3	20

Figure 5.5

It may be worth mentioning, that unless a series of BASIC programs are written to initially input data items, and then to update them when necessary, any alteration of data has to be done manually using the editing facilities. Even dictionary items have to be set up via the editor using 'insertion mode' But, since the editor can be controlled by a PROC, simple file alterations and dictionary creations can be quickly programmed and made almost idiot proof. There are many packages which are designed to help the user to input dictionary attributes by using the provided question and answer sessions.

The dictionary level of a data file is used to define the elements of the items in the associated data level of that file or another file. An item in a dictionary defines the attribute number, a title for the attribute, a left or right text justification and a column width for report generation. A dictionary item can convert data attributes such as dates, time and money into an understandable formatted output. In order to create logical relationships between data attributes, a dictionary item may also extract data from more than one file providing associations between data attributes, manipulating data attributes, the merging of two data attributes to produce a new piece of information, or combinations of these features. The use of this dictionary structure allows many complex logical relationships between data to exist, making a truly relational database management system.

The dictionary facility makes it possible to generate one complete description of the total database, and many sub- descriptions to delineate data structures for a specific area of application. These dictionary facilities make a wide variety of reports easy to generate, thus simplifying the control of a database. Also having these facilities allows *ad hoc* reporting to be done without having to write a program. It is the manipulation of these dictionary items which leads to Pick becoming an information system and a decision support system.

Chapter 6

The Master Dictionary

What is an Account?

In any business there are a number of distinct functions which are performed within an organisation. Each of these tends to utilise a different set of files. In conventional office practice each function would have its own set of filing cabinets. The sales office may have files on each of its customers in one drawer, and territory records for each of the salesmen, (for measuring performance), in the next drawer. Each drawer in a filing cabinet is equivalent to one data file stored on the Pick system.

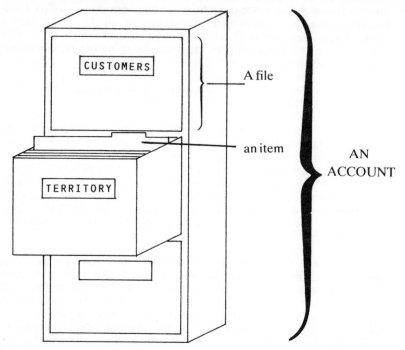

Figure 6.1   A departmental filing cabinet.

An account is a computerised filing cabinet, separating 'sets' of data from different departments. The SALES account contains two files, TERRITORY and CUSTOMERS which are shown in figure 6.2.

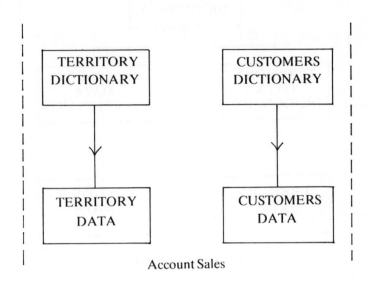

Account Sales

Figure 6.2 Where ----- represents the boundary of the account

Both of the sales files reside in the same account and, in order to make them both accessible, a master dictionary is used to control them. Figure 6.2 changes to Figure 6.3, with the master dictionary connected to the sales files.

The master dictionaries comprise the next level in the file hierarchy. Each user account has only one of these dictionaries associated with it, and in the majority of cases this dictionary will be unique. In some companies, the accounts may be divided into two parts - one part containing the ledgers and the other stock control and order entry. In this case, the master dictionaries for the two different users would be similar rather than unique. Uniqueness is achieved by adjusting account vocabularies to the needs of a specific user. Any sensitive commands, such as delete, can be omitted from a given account, effectively preventing the use of that command.

The Master Dictionary or MD as it is referred to, contains entries that describe all the available user commands, as well as describing the files which can be accessed. In Figure 6.3 the MD has authority to give access to the TERRITORY file and the CUSTOMER file.

61

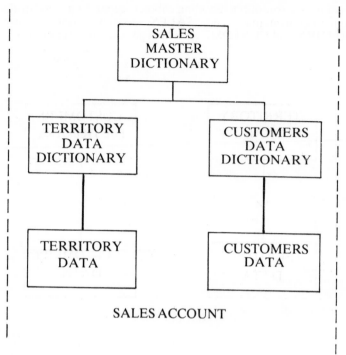

Figure 6.3

As well as the single commands (called verbs) the dictionaries can contain procedures, which store a series of commands: the commands may include Access language vocabulary.

As at the previous levels, the master dictionary is a file comprised of a number of items. Each of these items consists of a number of attributes, and all of these elements are infinitely variable in length. One of the functions of a master dictionary is to define what files can be accessed in the lower levels of the hierarchy. This function of the master dictionary is known as the file definition.

File Definition Items

As in the data dictionaries, which define the data in the level below them, the master dictionary is defining which files can be accessed in the lower levels. As might be expected, each of the attributes in these items have different meanings to the items in the data dictionary! So, let's have a quick look, just to get an appreciation of them and what they achieve. The dictionary item below is an example of a file definition item:

```
        TERRITORY
001  D
002  48480
003  7
004  1
005
006
007
008
009  L
010  10
```

The attributes have the following meanings:

Attribute 0

In this case the item identifier has to be the name of the file that is being pointed to.

Attribute 1

This is the D-code attribute; it must contain a D followed optionally by a one or two character code. When a file is first created a D is placed in this attribute. Other forms include:

DX   Do not save this file when saving the contents of an account.

DY   Do not save the data but the file space and structure remains.

DC   The file contains data in 0's and 1's (binary). Used by BASIC files. This type of file should not be accessed unless you're sure of what you're doing.

Attribute 2

This is the actual position of the file on the disk storage rather than the relative position in the next level of file. This figure allows the operating system to locate the position of the file ready for data retrieval.

Attributes 3 and 4

These two attributes give the internal structure of the file. Each file, when it is created, is divided into a number of smaller units. Each of these units is called a group, and is represented by a number in attribute 3, known as the modulo. The fourth attribute is known as the separation. These numbers represent the number of frames found in each group. A frame is a part of a group consisting of 512K. It is these portions of a file that are used in Pick's virtual memory. Virtual memory management enables the user to work with an area as large as all storage associated to the system. The actual core of the operating system is very small, so data files and program files are transferred in frames, as required from disk storage to main memory. This is done by the operating system through the use of a paging technique. In the example there are seven groups, each consisting of one frame.

The purpose of dividing a file into smaller units is to enable a search for a single item of data to take the shortest possible time. This process of defining modulo and separation for a file can be used to optimise the file accessing procedure. Programs are available to help choose the optimum combination of modulo and separation. Since the search for any one item is restricted to a single group, it is the group size and not the file size that will determine the speed and efficiency of data retrieval.

Attributes 5 and 6

These contain data update and retrieval passwords respectively, which are requested when a file is first created.

Attributes 7 to 10

These are the same as the attributes described in the previous chapter on data dictionaries. Usually only attributes 9 and 10 are used, the others being left null.

Synonyms for Files

File synonyms are used to allow access to files in another account. For example, the sales people may want to look at the current invoices for a specific customer. In the traditional office this would involve looking at a file in another filing cabinet, possibly in another office. Pick gives the ability to look at selected information in someone else's filing cabinet, and to set up signposts to the required data.

By having the ability to look in someone else's filing cabinet the objective of "data only being recorded once and shared by the various users of the system" is fulfilled.

These file synonyms are only found in the master dictionary. Again they have the general structure of a data dictionary item but with a few differences:

Attribute 1

This is still called the D-code attribute but must contain the character 'Q'!

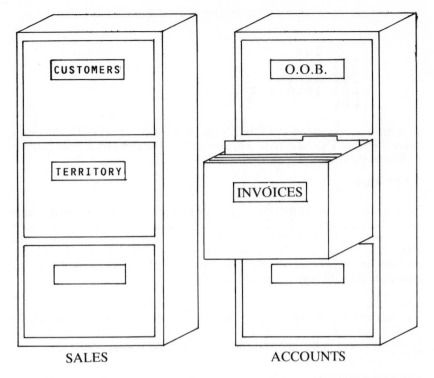

Figure 6.4 By using synonyms, accounting can make invoices available to the sales team, without having duplication of data.

Attribute 2

This contains the name of the account in which resides the file to be accessed.

Attribute 3

This contains the item identifier of the file to be accessed in the specified account

Attribute 4

This attribute is not used and should be left null.

Attributes 5 to 12

These have the same attributes to those used in file definition items.

For example, here is a synonym entry in the *sales* master dictionary:

```
      INV
001   Q
002   ADMIN
003   INVOICES
004
```

It permits access to the INVOICES file in the account ADMIN, by simply using the word INV as a verb. The contents of the INVOICES file could be looked at by using the command:

LIST INV

You may have noticed that there are only four attributes present in this item, when there are a potential 12. If only the first few are present in the item, the remaining can be omitted completely. This can be seen in dictionary item INV. The actual file definition item containing the physical location, modulo and separation is never duplicated, but always fetched from the owning master dictionary, in this case ADMIN.

The master dictionary not only contains file definition items for the files in that account, but also points to other files in other accounts. If Figure 6.5 is examined, the user of the SALES account has the ability to look at three files - two contained in the account and one in the ADMIN account.

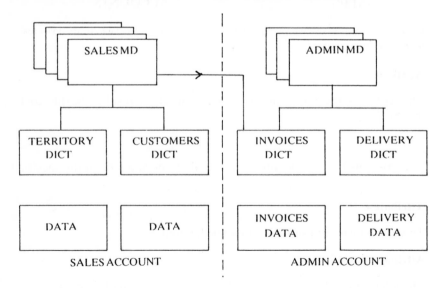

Figure 6.5

The file pointers can reference any data file or dictionary in the system, making all files available to any other user given the correct permission. Other files in the same account remain closed and secure. In the ADMIN account while the DELIVERY file remained secure from any unauthorised access.

The master dictionary defines the locations of files and also contains all the commands that can be executed directly from the terminal, these commands have been categorised and called Terminal Control Language (TCL).

Terminal Control Language

The terminal control language of the Pick operating system is the point of contact between the terminal user and the various pieces of the Pick jigsaw, as represented in Figure 6.6

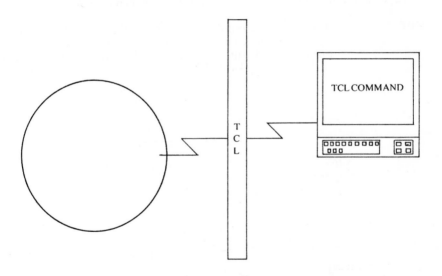

Figure 6.6 TCL, The "middleman" between the user at a terminal and Pick

TCL is present on each and every terminal at system start-up prior to a user logging on, but until the correct password has been given no command other than logon is valid. Once the user is logged on to his/her account, the full TCL vocabulary is invoked and further interaction and conversation with the machine is obtained.

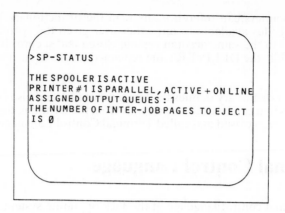

Figure 6.7

As well as dealing with peripherals, there are various user information verbs, which come under the category of utilities, which include:

WHO   Prints the line number that the terminal is connected to, and the account name to which the terminal is currently logged on. In Figure 6.8 we can see the various replies when each terminal asks WHO?

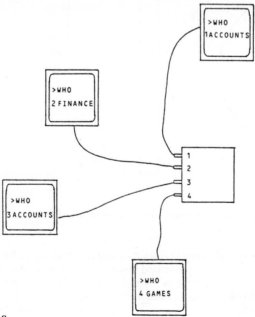

Figure 6.8

WHAT   Outputs the system status and configuration information.

TIME   This displays the current system time and date, as shown in Figure 6.9.

```
>TIME
14:27:42 15 MAY 1985
>
```

Figure 6.9

Other utilities allow the use of the Pick operating system as an incredibly expensive calculator. Verbs such as ADDD, MULD and SUBD are available There are also facilities to use the machine as a hexadecimal calculator, should the need ever arise. With these commands there is no facility for calculations in mixed bases (e.g. adding 21 (octal) to 39C (hexadecimal) and obtaining the answer in decimal.)

Also, messages can be sent between terminals using the command **MESSAGE**.

As can be seen none of these verbs allow access to a specified file.

2. Referencing verbs.

This group of commands allows a single file to be referenced. Many of these commands provide "gateways" into another part of the operating system. For example:

BASIC BP UPDATE

will activate the Pick DATA/BASIC compiler, compiling the item UPDATE which is in the file BP.

EDIT BP UPDATE

This invokes the editor, ready for altering item UPDATE in file BP.

When compilation or alteration of the item UPDATE has been completed control will be returned to TCL, indicated by the cursor prompt '>'.

3. Access Vocabulary

Access statements have a very flexible and generalised syntax with the ability only to specify a single file and to select a subset of that single file using items defined in the data dictionary associated with that file. An example statement would be:

```
SORT CUSTOMERS WITH DISCOUNT GT 5% DISCOUNT
PURCHASES
```

All the Access words in the statement (SORT, WITH and GT) will be defined in the master dictionary. The others being descriptions of pieces of data (DISCOUNT and PURCHASES) will be defined in the data dictionary for the file CUSTOMERS.

The verb itself has to be the item identifier or attribute 0. If we look at the contents of a master dictionary item for a Access verb, the attributes will be as follows.

```
000 SORT
```

Attribute 1 must contain the character P followed by another alphabetic character. This second character is used by the processor which works on the command. For instance any Access verbs will have the letters PA.

```
        SORT
001  PA
```

The SORT verb looks as shown above.

The remaining attributes define the starting point within the piece of the operating system that is being invoked.

This type of information is often interesting to know, but must never be altered. This is one of the reasons the EDIT command is often excluded from a user's master dictionary, in order to prevent loss of systems functions and business data.

The entire master dictionary user for SORT will be:

```
        SORT
001 PA
002 35
003 4E
```

Summary of TCL

TCL is a language which provides the assignment of the following resources:

Direct computation.

Processor assignment (e.g. ACCESS, EDITOR, BASIC.).

Modification of system characteristics.

Statistics on data and its distribution.

File creation.

TCL is rather like the command processor found in the operating system such as MS-DOS. There is a great deal to TCL, including commands for creating files and new accounts, setting the time and being better informed of the time and date, clearing files of data and sending messages to other users. For the user TCL does not appear as a separate entity but tends to blend in with the PROC and ACCESS parts of the operating system.

A complete list of TCL verbs found in the master dictionary is to be found in Appendix A

Procedures - PROCs

PROC stands for Stored Procedure. The PROC part of the operating system allows the user to pre-store a complex sequence of operations in one item, which can then be invoked by a single word command issued from TCL. Any sequence of operations that can be performed in TCL can be pre-stored and executed from a PROC. This is particularly useful for reports, where a library of items can be built up and run when needed, without having to type in a long string of commands, or complex Access statement.

One of the powerful features of the PROC language is a series of commands that make it easy to set up a formatted screen. With PROCs you can set screen characteristics, position the cursor, display screen prompts and check that any input from the keyboard is valid.

These Procedures are usually stored in an item in the user's master dictionary, and are items just like any other in the Pick operating system in that they consist of a variable number of attributes. The item-id is the name of the procedure and attribute 1 must contain the characters "PQ", which signals that the following attributes are to be passed to the PROC interpreter. Once stored, the Procedure becomes a command invoked by the item- id.

How a PROC works

PROCs use four buffers. These buffers are divided into two pairs, each consisting of one input buffer and one output buffer. Only one of the pairs are active at any one time.

These are represented diagrammatically as follows:

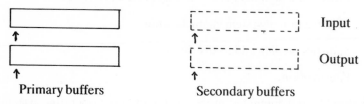

Primary buffers   Secondary buffers

Figure 6.10

In our case the active pair of buffers has been indicated by a solid line rather than a dotted line. Each buffer has a pointer (indicated by an arrow) which points to the position that is currently being looked at. All the pointers are initially set to position 0.

Each procedure is an item in a file, usually the master dictionary. Below is item LUCKY from file MD (Master Dictionary)

```
        LUCKY
001  PQ
002  RI
003  RO
004  HSORT
005  IP?
006  A
007  P
```

Let us use this example to see how the buffers actually operate.

Each PROC is stored as an individual item. In the above example the item-id is LUCKY. The first attribute value is always the code PQ. This specifies to the Pick system that what follows in the current item is to be handled by the PROC part of Pick. All the other attribute values contain statements that generate TCL comands or manipulate the contents of the buffers. PROC statements consist of an optional numeric label, a PROC command (usually of one or two letters), and then the data which the command is to use. Using some of the commands in LUCKY:

RO   This is just a two lettered command.

HSORT The 'H' is the PROC command, and SORT is the data used by 'H'.

Before the procedure is executed the four buffers may contain data from the last time they were used. There is only one set of buffers per system, looking like:

Figure 6.11

R I and R 0 commands will clear the input and output buffers giving:

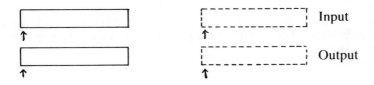

Figure 6.12

HSORT, causes the text SORT to be placed in the active output buffer. H is simply the command being used.

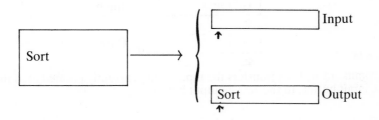

Figure 6.13

I P? then outputs a prompt to the user at the terminal. The answer that is required is the name of a file required to be sorted. This process is shown in Figure 6.14

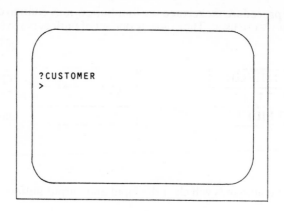

Figure 6.14

The user types in the file name, in this case CUSTOMER and presses "carriage return". This input is then placed in the currently active input buffer.

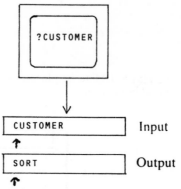

Figure 6.15

The command **A**, then transfers the input string currently pointed at in the active input buffer, to the active output buffer.

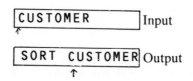

Figure 6.16

P then passes everything that is stacked in the output buffer to the Access processor for execution.

Figure 6.17

As is now clear the buffers act as temporary storage units for the collection of data before it is passed to its destination. When all the information required has been collected and is in the correct sequence it is released to another part of the operating system. If the example LUCKY is looked at the verb SORT, followed by its parameters, is collected in the buffers and then passed to the Access part of the operating system for execution. When execution is completed control, is passed back to the PROC.

In fact, some of the verbs which are used in TCL are actually procedures, such as utilities, for implementing saves, systems diagnostics and system statistical evaluations.

A few examples are :

```
SAVE
COMPARE
LOOP-ON
LISTDICT
LISTPROCS
LISTACC
LISTFILES
LISTUSERS
```

These PROCs come ready-made when the account is initially created. Any other PROCs developed by the individual, such as example LUCKY, is written and input by utilising the Editor. As with data dictionary items, there are many software packages which are designed to help the novice to create and run PROCs.

PROC features include:

1. An interactive mode of working, allowing prompting of the user at a terminal.

2. The transmission of arguments and parameters to other parts of the operating system.

3. Pattern matching and value tests. These give the ability to test and verify input data as it is entered from the terminal keyboard.

4. Conditional and unconditional branching using the optional labels and the IF statement.

5. Optional command labels giving each line a special number that can be used for locating the line quickly and easily.

6. Inter PROC linking. One PROC may call another. Once a PROC is invoked it will remain in control until it terminates, then it returns to TCL. This is seen in figure 6.18.

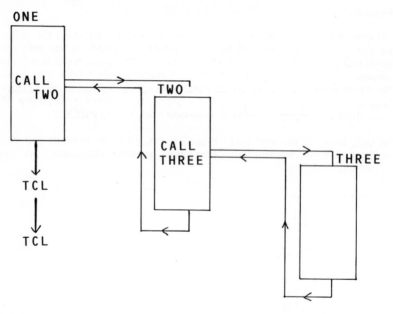

Figure 6.18

More importantly, PROC controls the system and its peripheral units by monitoring the status codes of the system

The PROC language is used to automate repetitive and complex sequences of interaction with various parts of the operating system. It is one of the most important software tools available within the operating system. It allows for speedy development of customized commands, which are especially useful for those who are not regular computer users. A complete list of the PROC commands is given in Appendix B

Chapter 7

The Control of the System

The system dictionary is the highest level of the PICK operating system file hierarchy. The whole hierarchy can now be revealed as consisting of four levels as seen in Figure 7.1.

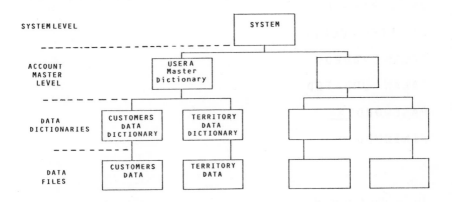

Figure 7.1 The four levels of files

There is only one system dictionary per operating system, which is shown on the diagram, and has an eagle eye over everything below it, not unlike a managing director as represented in an organisational chart. The major purpose of the system dictionary is to link together all existing accounts, and to store data about the accounts in one central place.

Each account has a unique identifying item stored in the system dictionary. It is initially created when an account is placed on the machine by using the CREATE-ACCOUNT verb.

For example, if the account ALAN was to be created the following question and answer session would take place:

```
>CREATE-ACCOUNT

ACCOUNT NAME?ALAN

L/RET-CODE(S)?

L/UPD-CODE(S)?

PRIVILEGES?SYS2

MOD,SEP?

CREATE-FILE(DICT ALAN 29,1)

[417]FILE 'ALAN' CREATED; BASE = 13534, MODULO =
29,SEPAR = 1

246 ITEMS COPIED

'ALAN' ADDED

'ALAN' UPDATED

PASSWORD?AJ

FINISHED

>
```

In the above example:

Upper case characters = machine prompt.
Underlined characters = user reply.
No user reply = a default value has been accepted by simply pressing carriage return.

The above creates the account 'ALAN' and places the following dictionary item in the system dictionary.

```
            ALAN
     001  D
     002  13534
     003  29
     004  1
     005
     006
     007  0C21BB1B
     008  SYS2
     009  L
     010  10
```

The attributes in a system dictionary item are as follows:

Attributes 1 to 4

These are the same as those found in the file dictionary definition held in the third level down in the hierarchy. The modulo and separation used at the point of creation are shown in attributes 3 and 4.

Attribute 5

This attribute contains a set of retrieval lock codes (enabling a file to be read) which are associated with the user. The only restriction is that they must be ASCII characters.

Attribute 6

This attribute contains a set of update lock-codes associated with the user.

Each file resident on the Pick operating system may be individually locked for both update and retrieval. A particular user might be assigned multiple codes for the set of files he is allowed to access. Using the code locking feature, a complex sequence of security and protection can be constructed for each user. During the use of an account, whenever a retrieval or update code is encountered, a search is made of the user assigned codes for a match; if no match is found then access to the file is denied.

Security codes are verified by comparing the value in the file dictionary against the corresponding string of values in the user identification item in the system dictionary. Characters are compared from left to right. So, we might have an account ALAN with the entry in the system dictionary as follows:

```
ALAN
001 D
002 3622
003 29
004 1
005 YES
006 YES
007
008 SYS2
009 L
010 10
```

Attributes 5 and 6 each have the update and read codes "YES". In order to look at a file it must also carry the same update and retrieval codes in attributes 5 and 6 of the dictionary file item.

For example, we could have two files in the account ALAN, called SALES and CUSTOMER, with the two file definition items in the master dictionary as follows:

```
        SALES                   CUSTOMER
001 D                   001 D
002 4508                002 3777
003 3343                003 223
004 1                   004 1
005 NO                  005 YES
006                     006 YES
007                     007
008                     008
009 L                   009 L
010 25                  010 10
```

When user 'ALAN' is trying to look at some information in the files, the retrieval codes in his user item are checked against the user items in the dictionary item of the file concerned. So the statement LIST SALES will result in:

[201] FILE 'SALES' IS ACCESS PROTECTED

as the two access codes do not match.

USER ID CODE	FILE DICT CODE	RESULT
YES	YES	Match - access allowed
NO	YES	Access denied
Y	YES	Access denied
YES	Y	Match - access allowed

As can be seen from the above table, the file dictionary code only need be part of the user identification code for the match to take place. Access is denied if the required password is incomplete (see line 3, in the above example).

A very complex pattern of file codes can be built up.

Attribute 7

This contains the user's password, to allow access to the requested account. As the account dictionary item can be looked at, the password is usually hash-coded to prevent unauthorised access to a protected account. Earlier when the account ALAN was being created, in answer to the password question a reply of AJ was made. When hashed it becomes OC21BB1B. A password is not compulsory.

Attribute 8

Contains a code indicating the level of privileges allowed to the user by the system. In the previous example both were awarded the SYS2 level. There are three levels of system privilege,

> SYS0
> SYS1
> and SYS2

SYS0 is the lowest form of privilege which gives the following restrictions:

1. No alteration to any Master Dictionary item. 2. No use of magnetic tape facilities. 3. No use of the DUMP verbs. 4. No use of DEBUG facilities. 5. No FILE-SAVE or FILE-RESTORE facilities.

This is the level of freedom that the user is automatically given, unless otherwise specified in the account creation procedure. When one of these categories of commands is used illegally then the following message is displayed:

`[82]YOUR SYSTEM PRIVILEGE LEVEL IS NOT SUFFICIENT FOR THIS STATEMENT`

Level SYS1 allows: updating and alteration of the master dictionary items.

Level SYS2 allows: the full use of all available facilities.

However, there are still some commands that can only be executed from the system programmers account SYSPROG, and these are listed in Appendix C.

Attribute 9

This may contain the code "U" which indicates that each time the user starts to and finishes using the system, the actual time of those two events is recorded by the system for accounting purposes.

Multiple User Accounts

File synonym items can be established in the system dictionary to allow multiple users to have access to the same account. In this case the concept of an account is a group of files, and the user is the individual with access to that set of files. The distinction can be used to allow multiple users, such as a group of people in an accounting department, to have controlled access to one particular set of files.

The file synonym definition item for each of these users points to the same master dictionary, but each user will have a separate password and system privileges level. Thus, some users might be able to access all of the file in an account while others may be restricted to two or three.

Entries in the system file define the user's master dictionaries, but also special files which are needed to control the system. These special files are known as system level files, and they are:

1. ACC These files are used for keeping track of the amount of time that users have used the machine.

2. BLOCK-CONVERT This file defines the format used when the characters are displayed in an enlarged format.

3. PROCLIB This file contains all the commonly used procedures such as LISTUSERS.

4. SYSTEM-ERRORS This file logs all the system errors that occur on the machine, giving a machine history.

There is also a special account which gives access to the user identification storage area, as well as the files containing the error messages, called SYSPROG.

By typing the word SYSPROG at the logon prompt, and the correct password, the key account to the system can be entered. Access to this account should only be given to a systems administrator as the SYSPROG account left in the hands of a novice can, and has been known to result in disaster. The special files are available to users when they need them. For example, the BLOCK- CONVERT file can be used via the BLOCK-PRINT command for printing out enlarged characters, such as:

```
      44
     444
    4444
   44 44
  44   44
444444444
     44
     44
```

by using the command BLOCK-PRINT 4, from the terminal.

The other files are not as directly usable, but they do come into use when a warning message is output, or when logging on and collecting the accounting information. The collected information must be protected from tampering.

System Usage Accounting

One of the standard files that constitutes the operating system software is the Accounting history file. This file is used by the operating system to accumlate statistics on each individuals use of the system's resources. It is divided into two sections: one part for "active users items", defining users who are presently active on the system; and one part for "accounting history items", defining past history.

Active user items include the name of the user, the port he was logged onto, and the amount of time he spent logged on. This data can be used to send messages to a specific person by finding the port on to which he is logged.

Accounting history consists of items that include the account name of the user as defined in the system dictionary, the channel or port number to which the user was logged on for that session, the date and time logged on, the total connect time, CPU charge units in tenths of a CPU second, and the number of pages that have been routed to the line printer.

Since the account history file is structured like any other file on the PICK system, the Access part of the system can be used to generate reports on system loading by port number, average connect time per user, average number of sessions per account and so on, as well as totals for customer billing or internal charging.

On the creation of a new account the master dictionary is copied from a limited set of the system dictionary.

The account information for each user in the system dictionary consists of the logon name, a logon password, and the file access codes for read and write privileges.

In the Pick operating system there are four distinct levels of security that protect the system and any data stored on the data base from unauthorised access. Each user is identified to the system by the user identification in the system dictionary. By establishing synonym definitions in the system dictionary, different levels of security can be assigned to different users logging on to the same account.

Before a user can log on, a password is requested. This password is stored in attribute 7 of the system dictionary, and can be as long or as short as required. This type of security is nothing new and is implemented on almost every type of computer system.

Since access is controllable on the file level as well as the system level, by the use of the retrieval and update codes, even the most complex security requirements can be easily satisfied by the PICK operating system. By individual assignment of passwords on a user by user basis and a corresponding file by file basis, careful control of the database use can be achieved in even the most dynamic computing environment. System security is also enhanced, in a generalised way, by the use of the three level restriction on the sensitive commands. Very sensitive commands are only present in the top SYSTEM level, and a password is required in order to enter that.

Chapter 8

The ACCESS Language

"Organisations create themselves according to their ability to use information."

R Stamper 1973

As was said earlier, information is the most important resource in any company, however large or small. In a small business, data held on a computer is usually financial. Even small businesses can have problems writing and preparing all their invoices and orders by hand, as well as controlling credit ratings of customers and the current position of stock. An analysis of any business will reveal that up to date information is the essential ingredient in all the decisions taken by a manager. How often has the following scenario happened on this high-tech fast-lane planet ?

Life in the Fast Lane

A number of managers are in an office discussing plans and budgeting for the company over the next couple of years. They need to look at some business figures in order to fuel both the arguments and the proposals. The only information these managers receive is to reconvene next week, by which time the computer will have been persuaded to yield the required information. One of two actions will take place. A decision will be made upon less information than is desirable, relying upon assumption rather than fact (which can lead to managers seeking new places of employment), or alternatively the meeting will be adjourned and continued a week later when the information is available (probably not the original information, but better this than have to wait yet another week!). This sort of prestigious computer is spending the company's money like water and providing the company with information worth only pence.

Information must not only be up to date, accurate and relevant, but also cost effective. A decision to raise the price of a tin of baked beans by two pence per can by a company producing 100,000 tin of beans a week, will be worthless if it costs the company more to produce the information in making the price increase decision than the revenues from the decision itself. Information must also be well presented and accurate. This can often be a nightmare for those personnel responsible for producing a management report.

The question that needs to be asked is: what exactly does management mean by well presented? Using Pick, obtaining a report for management presentation is no longer a nightmare. The Pick query language called Access, allows management to obtain reports containing the information they want, in the required format, exactly at the time they want it (every ten minutes if they are fanatical).

Procedural Languages

The Access query language is a non-procedural language. Retrieval languages may also be procedural, as examplified by COBOL, PASCAL, FORTRAN, ALGOL and BASIC (people either love or hate this type of language). They are procedural as the programmer has to define a foolproof sequence of events for the machine to complete. In a non-procedural language such as Pick's Access, the user doesn't have to go to the detailed lengths of writing programs, but merely expresses his wish or area of interest, leaving the machine's operating system to sort out the complex programming. In effect, constantly used routines have been preprogrammed and can be activated upon request. Another way of looking at this is to consider the actions necessary to produce a cup of tea. The instructions to your in-house robot might look something like this:

> Pick up kettle by the handle.
> Take off the lid.
> Put lid down on work top.
> Walk to the sink. Turn on the cold tap.
> Hold kettle under the running water.
> Wait 15 seconds.
> Take kettle away from running water.
> Turn off the cold tap.
> Walk to electric socket.
> Put kettle down on work surface.
> Replace lid. Insert electric cable into kettle.
> Switch kettle on.

This is procedural. Every time a cup of tea is requested, the robot would need to be given this sequence of instructions. The helpfulness of the robot would be minimal - you would be wasting more time telling the robot what to do than actually drinking tea. Alternatively by having a tea machine installed, and pressing the button labelled TEA, within 30 seconds or so a cup of tea (of sorts) arrives ready for drinking. This illustrates a non-procedural interface. You have told the machine you want a cup of tea, and then given a list of constraints: sugar, no sugar, milk and so on.

Using ACCESS

Access is a generalised information management and data retrieval language. A typical inquiry consists of a relatively free form sentence containing appropriate verbs, file names, data selection criteria and format modifiers. Access is, therefore, said to be a dictionary-driven language.

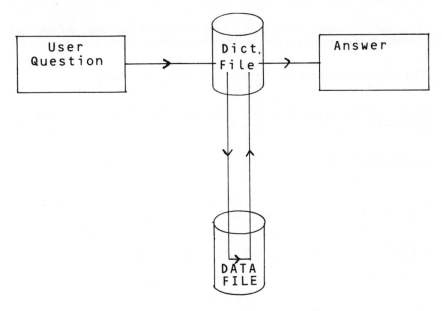

Figure 8.1

An access command is normally entered directly from the keyboard and sent to the processor by pressing the RETURN key. Unless otherwise specified the answer to the request for information will come back to the terminal. As seen in Figure 8.1 the user request travels via the data dictionary and the data file, selecting the required information, and then formatting it, before being displayed at the terminal. The structure of Access is close to standard English in that the commands are called verbs and are action commands. The most used verbs in access are:

      LIST
      SORT

As well as others including:

      COUNT
      HASH-TEST
      ISTAT
      LIST-LABEL
      SAVE-LIST
      SELECT
      SORT-LABEL
      SSELECT
      STAT
      SUM

The verb always has to be the first word in an access sentence. The second word of the command is usually the name of a file.

After the file name there may be a collection of various other criteria and commands making up a request tailored to each individual's requirement.

The simplest command is just a verb followed by a file name.

In this section the file VEHICLE is going to be used. (A complete listing can be found at the end of this section.)

LIST VEHICLE

This gives a display of all items in the file, listing the contents of certain pre-selected attributes from all of the records.

```
PAGE1          13:00:00 24 JAN 1985

VEHICLE...  REG....  SERVICE. MAKE
            NO       DUE
N3          A667CUA  03/01/84 10
N4          A675TYR  04/01/84 11
4613        B8800RW  04/02/85 14
6062        ABC125Y  01/03/85 44
0001        A951MBW  02/02/83 13
1097        RUR614D  24/04/85 17
N7          PLO630W  17/03/83 12
00004       LCC704P  27/06/68 19
N32         PAP121X  29/03/68 18
00007       PWW906W  01/02/83 18
N10         A735RYG  01/02/85 10
V2          B234THY  26/03/84 14
V3          JUB359V  01/06/83 44
4693                 05/02/85 99

14 ITEM LISTED
```

The LIST verb reads items from the file in sequential order, i.e. the order they are stored in. When the list is longer than the screen allows to be displayed at one time, the output process will halt at the end of each page and will not continue until the user gives the go-ahead by depressing the RETURN key. By using the command:

LIST VEHICLE NOPAGE

no depression of the RETURN key is necessary between the pages of display: the output is continuous. This command modifier was used mainly in the days when printing terminals were commonplace. This does not need to be used when outputting to a printer.

Each new item is automatically given a new line on the output, but to aid the easy reading of a report, double spacing can be requested. By using the statement,

LIST VEHICLE DBL-SP

the above listing becomes:

```
PAGE1           13:00:00 24 JAN 1985

VEHICLE...  REG....  SERVICE. MAKE
            NO       DUE
N3          A667CUA  03/01/84 10
N4          A675TYR  04/01/84 11
4613        B8800RW  04/02/85 14
6062        ABC125Y  01/03/85 44
0001        A951MBW  02/02/83 13
1097        RUR614D  24/04/85 17
N7          PLO630W  17/03/83 12
00004       LCC704P  27/06/68 19
N32         PAP121X  29/03/68 18
00007       PWW906W  01/02/83 18
N10         A735RYG  01/02/85 10
V2          B234THY  26/03/84 14
43          JUB359V  01/06/83 44
4693                 05/02/85 99

14 ITEMS LISTED.
```

As can be seen, when each report is activated a heading containing the page number, the time and the date is output as well as an end of list message containing a count of the number of items that have been printed. These can be suppressed using the modifier HDR-SUPP, leaving the listing consisting of the column headings and the lines of data. Even the column headings can be eliminated along with the time, date and page number by using the modifier COL-HDR-SUPP; resulting in just columns of data. The next example is produced by the statement:

```
LIST VEHICLE COL-HDR-SUPP

N3          A667CUA 03/01/84  10
N4          A675TYR 04/01/84  11
4613        B8800RW 04/02/85  14
6062        ABC125Y 01/03/85  44
0001        A951MBW 02/02/83  13
1097        RUR614D 24/04/85  17
N7          PL0630W 17/03/83  12
00004       LCC704P 27/06/68  19
N32         PAP121X 29/03/68  18
00007       PWW906W 01/02/83  18
N10         A735RYG 01/02/85  10
V2          B234THY 26/03/84  14
V3          JUB359V 01/06/83  44
4693                05/02/85  99
```

These modifiers can be combined as required, with as many as are necessary for the output requirements:

```
LIST VEHICLE COL-HDR-SUPP DBL-SPC NOPAGE
```

Each element of the access sentence must be separated by at least one space, so that the operating system can recognise them.

Having formatted the report as required, it is time to send the list to the line printer. This is achieved by adding the modifier LPTR or (P) to the end of the sentence.

```
LIST VEHICLE DBL-SPC HDR-SUPP (P)
```

This sentence will send a listing of the vehicle file, with the data lines double spaced, without any page headings and the end of list message to the printer.

Selection of Specific Attributes for Listing

In the data dictionary file for the VEHICLE file is a list of the words that can be combined with an Access verb to form a valid sentence.

Each word represents an item in the data dictionary. Each of these items defines the data: where it is kept, what it should look like when displayed and other features. By including one or more of these data dictionary items, the pre-defined set of attributes being displayed with LIST VEHICLE can be overridden. The words we have in the data for the VEHICLE file are:

```
COST
DEPARTMENT
DRIVER
FLEET NO
MAKE
MAKE.NAME
REG. NO
SERVICE.DUE
TAX.DUE.DATE
```

Any number of attributes, in any order, may be requested in an Access sentence. The fields may appear anywhere in the sentence, after the file name.

LIST VEHICLE MAKE MAKE.NAME REG.NO

PAGE 1   13:00:00 24 JAN 1985

VEHICLE...	MAKE	MAKE.................	REG.... NO
N3	10	FORD	A667CUA
N4	11	MERCEDES	A675TYR
4613	14	BRITISH LEYLAND	B8800RW
6062	44	PEUGOT	ABC125Y
0001	13	SAAB	A951MBW
1097	17	CITROEN	RUR614D
N7	12	VOLVO	PL0630W
00004	19	RENAULT	LCC704P
N32	18	VOLKSWAGEN	PAP121X
00007	18	VOLKSWAGEN	PWW906W
N10	10	FORD	A735RYG
V2	14	BRITISH LEYLAND	B234THY
V3	44	PEUGEOT	JUB359V
4693	99	SINCLAIR	

14 ITEMS LISTED.

The first column has displayed the item identifiers automatically, and this has a heading of the file we are looking at VEHICLE. If required the item identifiers can be suppressed with a output modifier ID-SUPP, seen in the next example. The other requested attributes are printed in the order they were input in the Access sentence.

```
PAGE1                    13:00:00 24 JAN 1985
REG....  DRIVER.............. DEPARTMENT
         NAME

A667CUA  KEVIN  BARRY           SALES
A675TYR  MARK  SUTTON           SALES
B8800RW  MARY  PAUL             ENGINEERING
ABC125Y  JOHN  LIONS            RESEARCH AND
                                DEVELOPMENT
A951MBW  JEAN  AISH             ENGINEERING
RUR614D  NICK  PHILLIPS         SALES
PL0630W  MIKE  MOULTON          MARKETING
LCC704P  STEVE  WHITTINGHAM     SALES
PAP121X  PETER  STEPHENSON      MARKETING
PWW906W  CHRIS  O'BYRNE         SALES
A735RYG  JIM  LAMLEY            SALES
B234THY  STEVE  WALTERS         MARKETING
JUB359V  STEPHEN  POTTER        SALES
         MARTIN  BONE           SALES
```

14 ITEMS LISTED.

John Lions, who has car ABC125Y, is in a department with a name longer
than the currently assigned column width of 20 characters, so instead of
truncating the data, Pick has continued the department's name on the next
line. The column widths are controlled for each dictionary item by attribute
10. Below is a listing of the contents of the dictionary item DEPARTMENT
from the example file VEHICLE.

```
                          DEPARTMENT
         Attribute  001   S
                    002   8
                    003   DEPARTMENT
                    004
                    005
                    006
                    007
                    008   TDEPARTMENT;C;;1
                    009   T
                    010   20
```

As can be seen the value in attribute 10 of the dictionary item DEPARTMENT contains 20 indicating the width of the column. In order to prevent the wrap round of data, the column width can be increased by altering attribute 10, to say 25. (The facilities of the Editor used for making the alteration can be found in a later chapter.)

```
        DEPARTMENT
001 S
002 8
003 DEPARTMENT
004
005
006
007
008 TDEPARTMENT;C;;1
009 T
010 25
```

On generating the report using the new version of the dictionary item, the following results are obtained:

VEHICLE REG.NO DRIVER DEPARTMENT ID-SUPP

PAGE1   13:00:00   24 JAN 1985

```
REG....  DRIVER..............  DEPARTMENT..............
         NAME
A667CUA  KEVIN BARRY           SALES
A675TYR  MARK SUTTON           SALES
B8800RW  MARY PAUL             ENGINEERING
ABC125Y  JOHN LIONS            RESEARCH AND DEVELOPMENT
A951MBW  JEAN AISH             ENGINEERING
RUR614D  NICK PHILLIPS         SALES
PLO630W  MIKE MOULTON          MARKETING
LCC704P  STEVE WHITTINGHAM     SALES
PAP121X  PETER STEPHENSON      MARKETING
PWW906W  CHRIS O'BYRNE         SALES
A735RYG  JIM LAMLEY            SALES
B234THY  STEVE WALTERS         MARKETING
JUB359V  STEPHEN POTTER        SALES
         MARTIN BONE           SALES
```

14 ITEMS LISTED.

This change to the dictionary item has resulted in the column being widened, but the data has remained unchanged. The defined width of the output column has no effect on the actual length of the value which is stored in the data file. The title has acquired a few more dots which act as padding characters to the true column width. Attribute 10 must always contain an integer.

Access has the ability to be selective, as listing the entire file in no particular order is not tremendously informative. How does a manager retrieve information in a more meaningful way ? Like the tea machine mentioned earlier, the operating system needs a little more information, for example "WITH TWO SUGARS", in order to obtain what you really want and not just a cup of tasteless steaming liquid. To clarify the request for information the Access sentence uses a series of options. Being a relational database the mechanics of the query language are based upon relational mathematics , which is hidden from the user in general, but comes to light when giving selection criteria. To select a subset of the VEHICLE file, the WITH modifier is used with a relational operator. These are:

EQ = NULL	} EQUAL TO
GT AFTER >	} GREATER THAN
LT BEFORE <	} LESS THAN
GE >=	} GREATER THAN OR EQUAL TO
LE <=	} LESS THAN OR EQUAL TO
NE NOT	} NOT EQUAL TO

Listed below are a few of the possible sentences that could be constructed using the above operators.

        LIST VEHICLE WITH DEPARTMENT EQ "SALES"

        LIST VEHICLE IF DEPARTMENT = "SALES"

        LIST VEHICLE WITH DEPARTMENT "SALES"

        LIST VEHICLE IF SERVICE.DUE AFTER "1 JAN 1984"

        LIST VEHICLE WITH NO REG.NO

Each of these give a selection of the entire file based on one constraint, but more than one item of selection may be used and combined in one sentence.

LIST VEHICLE WITH DEPARTMENT EQ "SALES" AND WITH NO REG.NO

This is achieved by using the logical connectives AND and OR which allows several criteria to be tested for simultaneously.

In addition. Access can search for values of a particular field, consisting of specified character or characters plus any others, by including square brackets inside the double quotes surrounding the value that is being searched for. This is useful on those occasions when the correct spelling is not known.

LIST VEHICLE WITH DRIVER = "M]" REG.NO DRIVER DEPARTMENT

The above example will find all drivers whose name begins with 'M' followed by any other characters, giving the result below.

```
PAGE    1                              13:00:00   24
JAN 1985

VEHICLE...          REG....           DRIVER.............
DEPARTMENT...............
                    NAME
N4          A675TYR MARK  SUTTON       SALES
4618        B8800RW MARY  PAUL         ENGINEERING
N7          PL0630W MIKE  MOULTON      MARKETING
4693                MARTIN BONE        SALES

4 ITEMS LISTED.
```

All the examples so far merely used the verb LIST, with various selection criteria and output modifiers to aid reporting. One of the verbs mentioned at the beginning of the chapter was the SORT verb. The verb SORT gives the name output as the LIST verb, as well as including the afore mentioned facilities. In addition, the items in the file may be displayed sorted in various ways. The command:

SORT VEHICLE

will give the same output as

LIST VEHICLE

but the records will be displayed in ascending order of value of the item identifier:

```
VEHICLE...  REG...    SERVICE.  MAKE
            NO        DUE
00001       A951MBW   02/02/83  13
00004       LCC704P   27/06/68  19
00007       PWW906W   01/02/83  18
1097        RUR614D   24/04/85  17
4613        B8800RW   04/02/85  14
4693                  05/02/85  99
6062        ABC125Y   01/03/85  44
N3          A667CUA   03/01/84  10
N4          A675TYR   04/01/84  11
N7          PL0630W   17/03/83  12
N10         A735RYG   01/02/85  10
N32         PAP121X   29/03/68  18
V2          B234THY   26/03/84  14
V3          JUB359V   01/06/83  44
```

14 ITEMS LISTED

The item identifier has been sorted by the left most character in the vehicle number. Whether to sort on the left-or right-most character is decided by looking at attribute 9 of the relevant data dictionary. Shown below is the VEHICLE item. As well as using attribute 9 for output justification it is also used for defining which character to sort upon.

```
            VEHICLE
001         D
002         42480
003         23
004
005
006
007
008
009         L
010         10
```

An ascending sort on values of any other dictionary item is achieved by including in the command the modifier BY, followed by the item name.

```
SORT VEHICLE BY REG.NO REG.NO DRIVER DEPARTMENT ID-SUPP

PAGE    1                              13:00:00 24 JAN 1985

REG....  DRIVER..............  DEPARTMENT...............
         NAME
         MARTIN BONE           SALES
ABC125Y  JOHN LIONS            RESEARCH AND DEVELOPMENT
A667CUA  KEVIN BARRY           SALES
A675TYR  MARK SUTTON           SALES
A735RYG  JIM LAMLEY            SALES
A951MBW  JEAN AISH             ENGINEERING
B234THY  STEVE WALTERS         MARKETING
B8800RW  MARY PAUL             ENGINEERING
JUB359V  STEPHEN POTTER        SALES
LCC704P  STEVE WHITTINGHAM     SALES
PAP121X  PETER STEPHENSON      MARKETING
PL0630W  MIKE MOULTON          MARKETING
PWW906W  CHRIS O+BYRNE         SALES
RUR614D  NICK PHILLIPS         SALES

14 ITEMS LISTED.
```

This gives a display sorted alphabetically by registration number of the car. Up to 15 sort criteria can be used in any Access statement.

```
SORT VEHICLE BY DEPARTMENT BY REG.NO DEPARTMENT REG.NO

PAGE    1                              13:00:00  24 JAN 1985

VEHICLE...  DEPARTMENT..............  REG....
                                      NO
00001       ENGINEERING               A951MBW
4613        ENGINEERING               B8800RW
V2          MARKETING                 B234THY
N32         MARKETING                 PAP121X
N7          MARKETING                 PL0630W
6062        RESEARCH & DEVELOPMENT    ABC125Y
4693        SALES
N3          SALES                     A667CUA
N4          SALES                     A675TYR
N10         SALES                     A735RYG
V3          SALES                     JUB359V
00004       SALES                     LCC704P
00007       SALES                     PWW906W
1097        SALES                     RUR614D

14 ITEMS LISTED.
```

First, all the departments have been sorted into alphabetical order, and secondly, within each category or department the registration numbers have been sorted into ascending order as can be seen more clearly in the extract below from the original report:

```
VEHICLE... DEPARTMENT.............. REG....
V2          MARKETING                   B234THY
N32M        MARKETING                   PAP121X
N7          MARKETING                   PL0630W
```

A descending sort may be specified by using the modifier BY-DSND in place of the BY. The BY-DSND and BY modifiers may be mixed freely in any Access sentence.

```
SORT VEHICLE BY DEPARTMENT BY-DSND REG. NO.
DEPARTMENT REG. NO.
```

Giving:

```
PAGE   1                    13:00:00   24 JAN 1985


VEHICLE... DEPARTMENT.............. REG....
                                          NO
4613        ENGINEERING                 B8800RW
00001       ENGINEERING                 A951MBW
N7          MARKETING                   PL0630W
N32         MARKETING                   PAP121X
V2          MARKETING                   B234THY
6062        RESEARCH AND DEVELOPMENT    ABC125Y
1097        SALES                       RUR614D
00007       SALES                       PWW906W
00004       SALESL                      CC704P
V3          SALES                       JUB359V
N10         SALES                       A735RYG
N4          SALES                       A675TYR
N3          SALES                       A667CUA
4693        SALES

14 ITEMS LISTED.
```

Other verbs include the COUNT verb which will simply give the result of counting the number of records in a file. The sentence:

```
COUNT VEHICLE
```

will return the number of records in the VEHICLE file:

```
14 ITEMS COUNTED
```

```
COUNT VEHICLE
```

will return the number of records in the VEHICLE FILE:

14 ITEMS COUNTED

The the sentence:

COUNT VEHICLE WITH DRIVER = "[TT]"

will only return those items meeting the criteria of having double "T" in the drivers name:

3 ITEMS COUNTED

The verb SUM will give the total of the values of a single element from all the records in the file which meet any conditions specified in the rest of the sentence. The command:

SUM VEHICLE COST

will return to screen the total of the COST element for all items in the file, while the command:

SUM VEHICLE COST WITH MAKE.NAME = "FORD"

will return the total of that element only for records whose MAKE.NAME consists of FORD.

The verb STAT will give more comprehensive calculations by giving the total of an element, as in SUM, the count, as in T verb, and the average.

All of these reporting formats are achieved by associating with each data file a dictionary file which contains coded information about the way various data elements are to be displayed. Associated with each data file is a dictionary file at the next level up in the hierarchy. The file dictionary contains controlling records which define the structure of the data in the data file. For example, an Access statement used earlier was:

LIST VEHICLE MAKE MAKE.NAME REG.NO

The 'word' MAKE refers to a particular element in the data record of the file VEHICLE, and this is defined by an item in the dictionary file, which specifies that MAKE is the second attribute in each data item, that it is to be displayed left justified in a column width of four characters, and so on.

```
        MAKE
001    A
002    2
003    MAKE
004
005
006
007
008
009    L
010    4
```

A special feature in Access is that it is possible to enter a sentence which does not require any data elements for display to be named. The operating system automatically outputs a default listing. In the case of

LIST VEHICLE

which was shown earlier in the chapter, the registration number, next service due and make were displayed

This is achieved by synonym file definitions being created in the data dictionary. These are exactly like ordinary dictionary items. Instead of having alphabetic names as item identifiers, such as REG.NO and MAKE, a series of numbers are used (starting from 1). On receiving the statement LIST VEHICLE the Access processor looks for a dictionary item with the item-id of 1, then a 2, then a 3 and so on. As soon as the next sequential number is not found the output of data items stops. When a named dictionary item is used, the numbered search is not actioned.

The VEHICLE file contains these three dictionary items:

	1	2	3
001	A	A	A
002	1	3	2
003	REG]NO	SERVICE]DUE	MAKE
004			
005			
006			
007			
008	D2/		
009	L	R	L
010	7	8	4

These produce the following listing from the statement:

```
LIST VEHICLE

PAGE   1                13:00:00 24 JAN 1985

VEHICLE...  REG....  SERVICE. MAKE
            NO       DUE
N3          A667CUA  03/01/84 10
N4          A675TYR  04/01/84 11
4613        B8800RW  04/02/85 14
6062        ABC125Y  01/03/85 44
00001       A951MBW  02/02/83 13
1097        RUR614D  24/04/85 17
N7          PLO630W  17/03/83 12
00004       LCC704P  27/06/68 19
N32         PAP121X  29/03/68 18
00007       PWW906W  01/02/83 18
N10         A735RYG  01/02/85 10
V2          B234THY  26/03/84 14
V3          JUB359V  01/06/83 44
4693                 05/02/85 99


14 ITEMS LISTED.
```

This default output is useful for producing a standard report, without having to type in all the dictionary names. Without the default, to obtain the same output the required statement would be:

```
LIST VEHICLE REG.NO SERVICE.DUE MAKE
```

The order of the numbers used as item identifiers does not bear any resemblance of the way in which the data is actually stored. These dictionary items are actually duplicate items going under another item-identifier, and are known as synonyms.

```
            1          REG.NO          REG
001         A          A               A
002         1          1               1
003         REG]NO     REG]NO          REG]NUMBER
004
005
006
007
008
009         L          L               L
010         7          7               7
```

Any number of synonyms can be created for a data item. This means that a user is not constrained to one 'keyword'. Different users may call the registration number REG.NO, REG or even 1 and obtain the same results. A dictionary can be a customised vocabulary for a specific user.

Conversions

Conversions are codes which are specified in the dictionary definition enabling data values to be held in a compact storage format, while remaining easily accessible for output in a suitable display form. The most common use for this facility is for storing dates and times. The way in which we express the date and time makes arithmetic very difficult to perform, and is often bulky to store.

Within the machine is an internal clock which counts the number of seconds from midnight during any one period of twenty four hours. The conversion codes refer only to the way that the data appears. They take effect at the time of the screen display or printing.

The most common use for conversion codes is the display of data which is entered in numeric form and must be displayed in certain format such as pounds and pence with a sign.

The available codes are:

```
MR
MR2
MR22
MR13
MR2,
```

The MR command justifies or aligns the numerics to the right. This is the normal way of aligning numbers in columns although if left justification is needed, the ML command is used instead.

The COST dictionary item gives the following output when the statement below is used.

VEHICLE...	REG..... NO	COST......
		2000
		3000
		3000
		25550
N3	A667CUA	2000
		3000
		1000
N4	A675TYR	
4613	B8800RW	1500
		3005
		2790
6062	ABC125Y	5250
		1500
		5250
00001	A951MBW	18679
		50000
1097	RUR614D	3000
		15368
		1327
		4576
N7	PLO630W	3500
00004	LCC704P	4500
N32	PAP121X	2398
00007	PWW906W	4500
		2310
		16754
		10000
N10	A735RYG	23089
V2	B234THY	129733
		3000
		6723
		8512
V3	JUB359V	
4693		4500
		1300

14 ITEMS LISTED

The following dictionary items can be associated with the VEHICLE data file, each showing a different output version of the COST data.

```
      COST                          COST-1
001   A                       001   A
002   9                       002   9
003   JOB]COST-S              003   COST-MR13
004                           004
005                           005
006                           006
007   MR                      007   MR13
008                           008
009   R                       009   R
010   9                       010   9
```

```
      COST-2                        COST-3
001   A                       001   A
002   9                       002   9
003   COST-MR2                003   COST-MR2C
004                           004
005                           005
006                           006
007   MR2                     007   MR2
008                           008
009   R                       009   R
010   9                       010   9
```

These dictionary items when used with the Access command

LIST VEHICLE COST COST-1 COST-2 COST-3

result in the following output:

VEHICLE...	COST.....	COST-MR2.	COST-MR13	COST-MR2C
	2000	20.00	2.0	20.00
	3000	30.00	3.0	30.00
	3000	30.00	3.0	30.00
	25550	255.50	25.6	255.50
N3	2000	20.00	2.0	20.00
	3000	30.00	3.0	30.00
	1000	10.00	1.0	10.00
N4				
4613	1500	15.00	1.5	15.00
	3005	30.05	3.0	30.05
	2790	27.90	2.8	27.90
6062	5250	52.50	5.3	52.50
	1500	15.00	1.5	15.00
	5250	52.50	5.3	52.50
00001	18679	186.79	18.7	186.79
	50000	500.00	50.0	500.00
1097	3000	30.00	3.0	30.00
	15368	153.68	15.4	153.68
	1327	13.27	1.3	13.27
	4576	45.76	4.6	45.76
N7	3500	35.00	3.5	35.00
00004	4500	45.00	4.5	45.00
N3	2239	823.98	2.4	23.98
00007	4500	45.00	4.5	45.00
	2310	23.10	2.3	23.10
	16754	167.54	16.8	167.54
	10000	100.00	10.0	100.00
N10	230089	230.89	23.1	230.89
V2	129733	1297.33	129.7	1,297.33
	3000	30.00	3.0	30.00
	6723	67.23	6.7	67.23
	8512	85.12	8.5	85.12
V3				
4693	4500	45.00	4.5	45.00
	1300	13.00	1.3	13.00

14 ITEMS LISTED.

The first column, headed COST, is the actual stored data displayed merely justified to the right. The other columns show alternative output formats for numbers.

In dictionary item MR2 the figure "2" in attribute 7 indicates how many figures will appear after the decimal point. It the data is stored to more decimal places than is indicated, then the conversion code will automatically round up or down before displaying the required number of decimal places. The stored number can also be descaled, by adding another conversion code. MR21 would divide the stored number by 10, MR22 divides the number by 100 and MR33, would divide the stored number by 1000. The decimal point and descaling codes work together, for instance MR13 will display a number with one decimal point, having descaled the original number by a factor of 1000. The result is rounded to one decimal point, as shown by the column labelled COST-MR13.

A comma can also be added after the decimal and descaling codes which will insert commas between the amounts of thousands, as shown in the example for MR2,

It is possible to add further complication (some say sophistication) to the output by including a minus sign for a debit (ideal for bank balances) or to include the symbol "(CR)" after the figure if it is in credit.

Dates

The date that is entered is stored as a string of numbers when a conversion code is used, and then has to be re-converted to appear in the right format when output. The number is calculated from the machine, starting to count from the 31st December 1967. The example below shows the internal numbers that are in the machine. Without a conversion into a more understandable format the data is almost useless. The dictionary item DATE, has no output conversion in attribute 7, so the original stored data is output.

`LIST VEHICLE DATE`

gives:

VEHICLE...	DATE....
N3	5847
N4	5848
4613	6245
6062	6270
00001	5512
1097	6324
N7	5555
00004	179
N32	89
00007	5511
N10	6242
V2	5930
V3	5631
4693	6246

The following dictionary items have been set up to show the different output formats:

```
        DATE       DATE-1        DATE-2        DATE-3
001  A          A             A             A
002  3          3             3             3
003  DATE       DATE-D2/      DATE-D-       DATE-
DO
004
005
006
007             D2/           D-            DO
008
009  R          R             R             R
010  8          8             8
```

Giving the shown result by using the statement:

```
LIST VEHICLE DATE DATE-1 DATE-2 DATE-3

VEHICLE.... DATE.... DATE-D2/ DATE-D-... DATE-DO
N3               5847 03/01/84  03-01-1984 01 JAN
N4               5848 04/01/84  04-01-1984 04 JAN
4613             6245 04/02/85  04-02-1985 04 FEB
6062             6270 01/03/85  01-03-1985 01 MAR
00001            5512 02/02/83  02-02-1983 02 FEB
1097             6324 24/04/85  24-04-1985 24 APR
N7               5555 17/03/83  17-03-1983 17 MAR
00004             179 27/06/68  27-06-1968 27 JUN
N32                89 29/03/68  29-03-1968 29 MAR
00007            5511 01/02/83  01-02-1983 01 FEB
N10              6242 01/02/85  01-02-1985 01 FEB
V2               5930 26/03/84  26-03-1984 26 MAR
V3               5631 01/06/83  01-06-1983 01 JUN
4693             6246 05/02/85  05-02-1985 05 FEB

14 ITEMS LISTED.
```

For example, let's look at the date 01/03/85 which is held internally 6270, and the attribute definition item DATE which contains the code in attribute 7. If an Access command is issued with the following format:

**SORT VEHICLE WITH SERVICE.DUE BEFORE "01/03/85"
BY DATE DRIVER REG.NO SERVICE.DUE**

In the processing of this sentence all the items in the VEHICLE file which meet the criteria 'before 1st January 1985' have to be selected. This is done by comparing each date attribute in the file with the specified date to see if it is less than the given date. The relational 'less than' has to be used. To enable the dates to be compared successfully and quickly they all need to be in the same format, the internal one.

```
            SERVICE.DUE
001    A
002    3
003    SERVICE]DUE
004
005
006
007    D2/
008
009    R
010    8
```

By placing the conversion code on attribute seven the specified value is converted into storage format, compared with every other internal SERVICE.DUE, and then converted into a readable, meaningful output format. In other words, the whole of the command is performed transparently to the user, on values in storage format.

The same date conversion code could be specified instead as a correlative, by simply placing the code in attribute eight of the dictionary item instead of attribute seven.

```
            SERVICE.DUE
001    A
002    3
003    SERVICE]DUE
004
005
006
007
008    D2/
009    R
010    8
```

Correlatives

All of this is very well, but currently we are simply using one file, which is not fulfilling the promise of a database, the relating of many files.

Where a particular data item can take one of only a few values, it would be wasteful of space to duplicate these values, since the information would be stored in possibly large numbers of records. For example, employee records in a department could be repeated thousands of times. The file translation code enables such values to be replaced by short code letters or numbers which are looked up in the dictionary file when output is required. This can be seen in the example earlier using MAKE and MAKE.NAME

VEHICLE...		MAKE.................	REG.... NO
N3	10	FORD	A667CUA
N4	11	MERCEDES	A675TYR
4613	14	BRITISH LEYLAND	B8800RW
6062	44	PEUGEOT	ABC125Y
00001	13	SAAB	A951MBW
1097	17	CITROEN	RUR614D
N7	12	VOLVO	PLO630W
00004	19	RENAULT	LCC704P
N32	18	VOLKSWAGEN	PAP121X
00007	18	VOLKSWAGEN	PWW906W
N10	10	FORD	A735RYG
V2	14	BRITISH LEYLAND	B234THY
V3	44	PEUGEOT	JUB359V
4693	99	SINCLAIR	

14 ITEMS LISTED.

In the dictionary file were two items MAKE and MAKE.NAME. The dictionary item MAKE was the actual value that was stored in the form of a two digit code between 00 - 99. The actual names of the make are held in another file called MAKES. This data is retrieved using a correlative at attribute 8 of the dictionary item, as shown below. The dictionary item MAKE just displays the make number, the dictionary item MAKE.NAME fetches some data from another file, relating the given number to a piece of text.

	MAKE.NAME		MAKE
001	S	001	A
002	2	002	2
003	MAKE	003	MAKE
004		004	
005		005	
006		006	
007		007	
008	TMAKES;C;;1	008	
009	T	009	L
010	200	010	4

So the displayed data is derived data which comes from another file in the system, giving 'data relating' abilities as shown in Figure 8.2

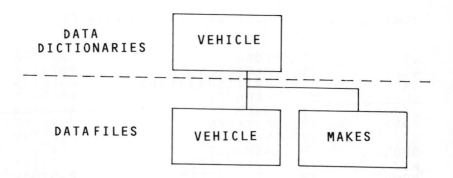

```
    DATA
 DICTIONARIES         VEHICLE


DATA FILES         VEHICLE          MAKES
```

Figure 8.2

How the TRANSLATE correlative works

The Access processor works its way down the dictionary item MAKE.NAME in the following way. Firstly it arrives at attribute 2, which indicates in any dictionary item which attribute in the data file is to be looked at. In this case attribute 2, which in the instance of data item N3 is equal to '10'. Attribute 8 is scanned and if a correlative is present, that is then processed. The statement held on attribute 8 of the dictionary item is

TMAKES;C;;1

The 'T' indicates that a translation from another file is about to take place. Directly following this is the file name MAKES. This file name is the file though which the translation takes place. The 'C' says "convert the value if possible, use the original value if the item in the MAKES file does not exist or has a null value." If item '10' did not exist in the MAKES file the output would be '10' as the translation could not take place. There are other alternatives to this which include having a blank output. The '1' indicates which attribute in the translate file to fetch and output according to the other output specifications given in the dictionary item.

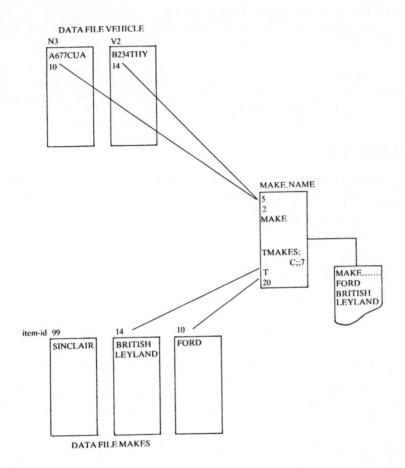

Figure 8.3

By using this translate facility, data duplication is avoided and changes in data can be made centrally in one file. An advantage of this facility is the saving of storage space. If, for example, credit ratings are kept on individuals in a file, many may well be repeated. Typical examples are:

> 30 days net
> 60 days net
> Pro Forma
> No Trading

111

Rather than have the phrase "30 days net" stored 80 times at 11 characters each, store a code, say 2. This will save 800 characters being stored. The two can then be translated to the full text on output.

A correlated attribute can be thought of as a ghost item. It does not occupy an attribute in its own right because the output value is borrowed. A correlative borrows data from elsewhere and in some cases derives a further value by manipulating the borrowed data. The correlated file derives its own value and does not need a value to be entered though the keyboard.

Summary

It can be seen that Access is a generalised information management and data retrieval language. A typical inquiry consists of a relatively free form sentence containing the appropriate verbs, files names, data selection criteria, and control modifiers. Access is a dictionary driven language with the following features:

1. The vocabulary used in composing an English-like sentence is contained in several dictionaries, each user's vocabulary being individually tailored.

2. Data files consist of a data section and a dictionary section.

3. The dictionary section contains the structural definition of the data section.

4. The Query language references the dictionary section for data field descriptions (hence the name dictionary!). These descriptions specify mnemonic names of data elements, functional calculations, inter-file retrieval operations, display formats and more. The Query language allows for selective or conditional retrieval of information.

5. Output reports are automatically formatted according to the user's specification and may appear on either a display terminal or a printer. The output may be sorted into any sequence defined by the user and includes the following extended features:

    (a) Relatively free-form input of word order.

    (b) Automatic or user specified output report formats in columnar or non-columnar forms.

    (c) Generalised data selection using relational and arithmetic relationships.

    (d) Sorting capability on a variable number of descending and ascending data items.

(e) Generation and retention of specially selected and/or sorted lists for future use.

(f) The ability of the user to define variables which are derived from the stored data, and then to search, select, sort total and output on the basis of the selection.

(g) Selection of subvalues within items containing multiple unit items.

(h) Generation of statistical information concerning the files held on the database.

A complete Access vocabulary list is to be found in Appendix A.

VEHICLE File Listing

The following pages show a complete listing of the VEHICLE file and related files that have been used in examples in this chapter.

VEHICLE FILE.
```
        N3
001  A677CUA
002  10
003  5847
004  1234
005
006
007  KEVIN BARRY
008  1
009  2000]3000]1000

        N4
001  A675TYR
002  11
003  5848
004  4321
005
006
007  MARK SUTTON
008  1
009

        4613
001  B800RW
002  14
003  6245
004  7654
005
006
007  MARY PAUL
008  3
009  1500]3005]2790

        6062
001  ABC125Y
002  44
003  6270
004  4567
005
006
007  JOHN LIONS
008  2
009  5250]1500]5250
```

```
      00001
001  A951MBW
002  13
003  5512
004  5847
005
006
007  JEAN AISH
008  3
009  1879]50000


      1097
001  RUR614D
002  17
003  6324
004  6624
005
006
007  NICK PHILLIPS
008  1
009  3000]15368]1327]4576


      N7
001  PLO360W
002  12
003  5555
004  6212
005
006
007  MIKE MOULTON
008  4
009  3050


      00004
001  LCC704P
002  19
003  179
004  479
005
006
007  STEVE WHITTINGHAM
008  1
009  4500
```

```
    N32
001 PAP121X
002 18
003 89
004 410
005
006
007 PETER STEPHENSON
008 4
009 3298

    00007
001 PWW906W
002 18
003 5511
004 6041
005
006
007 CHRIS O'BYRNE
008 1
009 4500]2310]16754]10000

    N10
001 A735RYG
002 10
003 6242
004 6342
005
006
007 JIM LAMLEY
008 1
009 23089

    V2
001 B234THY
002 14
003 5930
004 6210
005
006
007 STEVE WALTERS
008 4
009 129733]3000]6723]8512
```

```
        V3
001     JUB359Y
002     44
003     5631
004     5645
005
006
007     STEPHEN POTTER
008     1
009


        4693
001
002     99
003     6246
004     6301
005
006
007     MARTIN BONE
008     1
009     4500]1300
```

The above listing is how the items are displayed to the user on the screen, the listing below is how the data is actually stored, with no display spaces. Each " ^ " character that marks the end of an attribute causes a new line to be printed when being displayed.

```
N3^A667CUA^10^5847^1234^^^KEVIN BARRY^1^2000]3000]1000
N4^8675TYR^11^5848^4321^^^MARK SUTTON^1
4613^B8800BW^14^6245^7654^^^MARY PAUL^3^1500]3005]2790
6062^ABC125Y^44^6270^4567^^^JOHN LIONS^2^5250]1500]5250
00001^951MBW^13^5512^^^JEAN AISH^3^18679]50000
N7^PLO630W^12^12^5555^6216^^^MIKE MOULTON^4^3050
00004^LCC704P^19^179^479^^^STEVE WHITTINGHAM^1^4500
N32^PAP121X^18^89^410^^^PETER STEPHENSON^4^3298
00007^PWW906W^18^5511^6041^^^CHRIS O'BRYNE^1^4500]2310]16754]
1000
N10^A735RYG^10^6242^6342^^^JIM LAMLEY^1^23089
V2^B234THY^14^5930^6210^^^STEVE WALTERS^4^129733]3000]6723]8512
V3^JUB359Y^44^5631^5645^^^STEPHEN POTTER^1
4693^^99^6246^6301^^^MARTIN BONE^1^4500]1300
```

	REG.NO	MAKE	SERVICE.DUE	TAX.DUE.DATE
001	A	A	A	
002	1	2	4	
003	REG.NO	MAKE	SERVICE.DUE	TAX.DUE]DATE
004				
005				
006				
007				
008			D2/	D2/
009	L	L	R	R
010	7	4	8	8

Fig. 8.4 Contents of dictionary file VEHICLE

	DRIVER	COST	FLEET.NO	MAKE.NAME
001	A	A	S	S
002	7	9	0	2
003	DRIVER	COST	FLEET]NUMBER	MAKE]NAME
004				
005				
006				
007				
008			D2/	THAMES;C;;1
009	L	R	R	T
010	20	5	10	20

Fig. 8.5 Contents of dictionary file VEHICLE

	DEPARTMENT
001	S
002	8
003	DEPARTMENT
004	S
005	S
006	S
007	S
008	TDEPARTMENT;C;;1
009	T
010	20

DATA FILE DEPARTMENT

1^SALES
2^RESEARCH AND DEVELOPMENT

3^ENGINEERING
4^MARKETING

```
DATA FILE MAKES

10^FORD
11^MERCEDES
14^BRITISH LEYLAND
44^PEUGEOT
13^SAAB
17^CITROEN
12^VOLVO
19^RENAULT
18^VOLKSWAGEN
99^SINCLAIR
```

Chapter 9

The Editing Facilities

One of the most useful facilities for program development is an editor. An editor permits the insertion, amendment and deletion of individual characters, groups of characters or entire lines of a program. Editing in traditional computing is usually only applied to the source code of a program, but with the Pick operating system the editor can alter any item in any file which the user's account has access to.

Unless a series of BASIC programs are written to initially input data items, and then to update them when necessary, any alteration of data has to be done manually from the editor. This is dangerous as an inexperienced user can accidently corrupt data making the system useless. Even dictionary items have to be set up via the editor using insertion mode. But, since the editor can be controlled by a PROC, simple file alterations and dictionary creations can be quickly programmed and made almost idiot proof!

The editor is invoked by using the EDIT verb at TCL. All editor commands consist of one or two literal mnemonies followed by data for using with the command.

How the Editor Works

When the editor is first invoked from TCL, two images of the item concerned are created. To make this a lot clearer, let's look at an example:

```
      SERVICE.DUE
001   A
002   3
003   SERVICE]DUE
004
005
006
007
008   D2/
009   R
010   8
```

This is a dictionary item called SERVICE.DUE in the dictionary portion of the file VEHICLE.

Line 8 is displayed and a new prompt given. The current line can now be altered using any of the 'line' commands. In our case the replace command is used, demonstrated in Figure 9.5

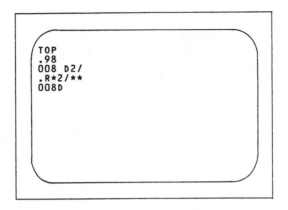

```
TOP
.98
008 D2/
.R*2/**
008D
```

Figure 9.5

The replace command (R*2 / **) substitutes nothing, (as that is what is between the second pair of asterisks), for the two characters contained between the first two asterisks, 2/. The change that the command effected will have been recorded in the second copy of the item, while the current screen version remains unaltered. This can be seen in Figure 9.6, by going to the top or beginning of the item (line 0) by using the command ' T ' and then ' L 10 '

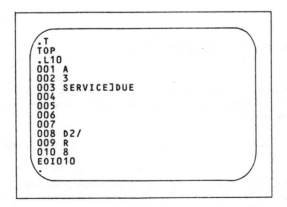

```
.T
TOP
.L10
001 A
002 3
003 SERVICE]DUE
004
005
006
007
008 D2/
009 R
010 8
EOI010
.
```

Figure 9.6

123

The two versions of the items look as follows:

current version
on screen,

second, machine
held version.

```
     SERVICE.DUE          SERVICE.DUE
001  A                001  A
002  SERVICE]DUE      003  3
003  SERVICE]DUE      003  SERVICE]DUE
004                   004
005                   005
006                   006
007                   007
008  D2/              008  D
009  R                009  R
010  8                019  8
```

To be able to see the changes that have been made the current version and the machine held second version have to be swapped. This is achieved by using the command 'F' which copies the second version onto the screen 'current version'.

All editing must continue in ascending line number sequence until an 'F' command is entered, automatically updating the existing item and initialising the current to line 0 again.

The editor offers many facilities including the merging of lines from the same or other items; the location of a string in an item followed by the replacement of that string. The insertion and deletion of lines, and the storing of complex editing commands for use time and time again. The summary below gives an explanation of each of the available editor commands.

Summary of Commands

Editor commands consist of one or two lettered mnemonics each of which is briefly explained below to give a new user or a potential user an idea of what facilities are available.

A - Again. This command repeats the last locate (L) command that was issued.

AS - Alternate This command acts as an alternating switch
  Switch. which turns the Assembly listing format either on or off. Very rarely used except by expert programmers.

B - Bottom. This command takes the current line pointer and assigns it to the last attribute in the item being edited. For our example SERVICE.DUE the following is shown to happen in Figure 10.7. Ten lines of the attribute are listed, go to the beginning of the item, go to the bottom of the item. The EOI comment (End Of Item) indicates that the end of the item has been reached and the last attribute number is displayed, although the actual contents of the line are not.

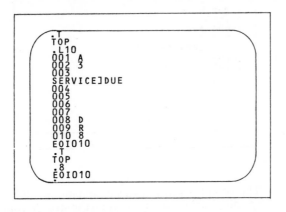

Figure 9.7

C - Column number list. This command prints out a list of column numbers so that the user can readily determine a columnar position of data in any given line.

DE - Delete. This command allows the deletion of a single line or a number of lines. The simplest form of the command is simply DE. This deletes the line currently being pointed to, as seen in Figure 9.8.

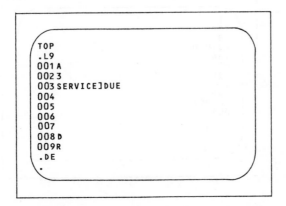

Figure 9.8

On inputting F, and then looking at the second version, it can be seen that the attribute where 'R' resided has been deleted and the remaining attributes re-numbered. Another command prompt is output. This sequence of events is displayed in Figure 9.9.

```
.DE
.F
TOP
.LIO
001 A
002 3
003 SERVICEJDUE
004
005
006
007
008 D
009 8
EOI009
.
```

Figure 9.9

The complex form of this command involves searching for a specified string, and then when the string is found the attribute concerned is deleted. If Figure 9.10 is studied the deleting command is . DE99/R/, entered at the top of the item. This command will search the next 99 lines, in our case, the entire item, for the string -R+. There are two such occurrences which when found are deleted. The line numbers deleted are displayed before the next command prompt.

```
.T
TOP
.B
EOI010
.G4
004
.DE
.F
TOP
.DE99/R/
003
.F
.L10
```

Figure 9.10

126

EX - Exit. This command quits the editor without saving any alterations that may have been done on the item. Invaluable when the wrong lines have been accidently deleted!

F This command switches the current screen version and the machine held second version of the item being edited. This allows the user to see what changes he has made, what affect they have had and what they actually look like. This is one of the basic commands needed for use of the editor.

FD-File This deletes an entire item in a file. For this reason, the editor should not be available for general use, in order to protect a business from either accidental or deliberate loss of data. Alteration of items is usually only allowed via a PROC or a BASIC program which is password protected.

In Figure 9.11 the deletions via the editor are shown, followed by an Access statement asking for a list of items in the dictionary, SERVICE.DUE is no longer present.

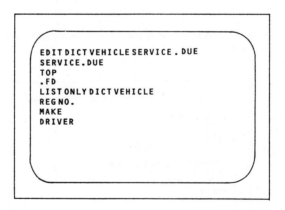

```
EDIT DICT VEHICLE SERVICE . DUE
SERVICE.DUE
TOP
.FD
LIST ONLY DICT VEHICLE
REG NO.
MAKE
DRIVER
```

Figure 9.11

FI-File item The item that is currently being edited is made permanent and filed away on disk, replacing the old version or, if it is a newly created item, creating a first version. The terminal returns to a TCL prompt as the editor is exited.

FS-File save The item that is currently being edited is made permanent by being filed away as in the command FI. The difference is that the user is still in the editor, with the current line set to the beginning of an item.

G - Goto.   This command must be followed by the number of the line that you wish to make current, shown in Figure 9.12.

```
EDIT DICT VEHICLE SERVICE.DUE
SERVICE.DUE
TOP
.63
003 SERVICE]DUE
```

Figure 9.12

I - Insert.   This command will insert any number of lines after the line that is currently active.

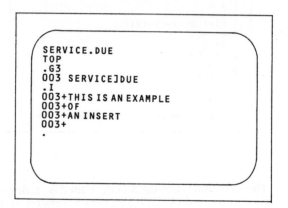

```
SERVICE.DUE
TOP
.G3
003 SERVICE]DUE
.I
003+THIS IS AN EXAMPLE
003+OF
003+AN INSERT
003+
.
```

Figure 9.13

In Figure 9.13 three lines have been inserted. The insert is terminated by <CR>. The new version is seen in Figure 9.14 after an ' F ' and a ' L6 ' command.

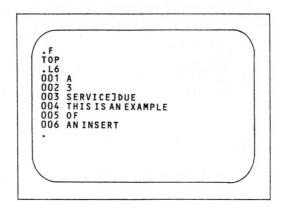

Figure 9.14

There are two versions of LIST:

1. L - List. This command will list the specified number of lines. (See Figure 9.15)

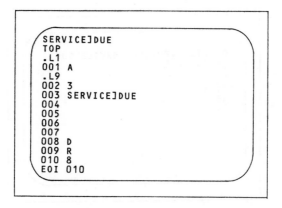

Figure 9.15

1. L-Conditional list. The LIST command contains a sequence of characters for which the command searches the item, and then lists the attributes containing that sequence. In Figure 9.16, the current line is at the *top* of the item when the command **L99/R/** is entered. This searches the next 99 lines for the character R, those found are then listed. The current line is the bottom of the item.

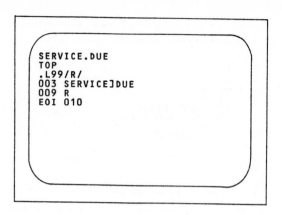

```
SERVICE.DUE
TOP
.L99/R/
003 SERVICE]DUE
009 R
EOI 010
```

Figure 9.16

ME - Merge. This command allows a specified number of lines to be copied into the item being edited, from any other item on the Pick system.

N - Next. This command increases the current line pointer by the number of specified lines, shown in Figure 9.17.

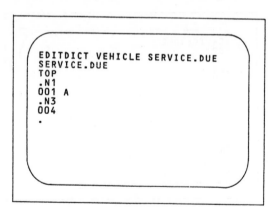

```
EDITDICT VEHICLE SERVICE.DUE
SERVICE.DUE
TOP
.N1
001 A
.N3
004
.
```

Figure 9.17

P - Prestore and prestore recall. The PRESTORE command allows a sequence of commands to be stored for repeated use. Up to 10 prestored sequences are allowed at any one time, very much like having ten memories on a calculator.

P or P0 is preprogrammed on every new Pick machine with the command L22, which displays a screen-full of attributes from the item.

To recall a sequence of commands that are already stored merely type in the command P followed by the number assigned to that sequence of prestored commands.

Any prestored commands can be displayed using PD

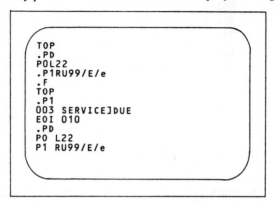

```
TOP
.PD
POL22
.P1RU99/E/e
.F
TOP
.P1
003  SERVICE]DUE
EOI  010
.PD
PO  L22
P1  RU99/E/e
```

Figure 9.18

In Figure 9.18 the current prestored items are displayed, and then P1, a replace command is input.

R - Replace. Replace has the ability to change an entire line or just a specified part of the line. In Figure 9.19 a replacement is made to the column heading in attribute 3. The character] is replaced by]NEXT, with / being used as the delimiter. The delimiter can be any non alphanumeric character, usually a ?, / or *. An asterisk replacement can be seen in Figure 9.5.

```
TOP.93
003  SERVICE]DUE
.R
003  DATE OF]SERVICE
.F
TOP
.93
003  DATE OF]SERVICE
R/]/]NEXT
003  DATE OF]NEXT  SERVICE
.F
TOP
.L3
001  A
002  3
003  DATE OF]NEXT SERVICE
```

Figure 9.19

T - Top. This takes you to the top of the item, ready to edit the attribute lines in ascending order.

131

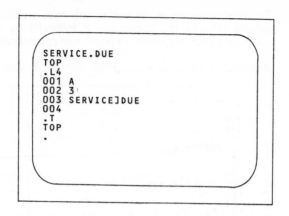

```
SERVICE.DUE
TOP
.L4
001  A
002  3
003  SERVICE]DUE
004
.T
TOP
.
```

Figure 9.20

TB - Tabs.   Tabs for spacing and easy editing can be preset. There can be up to 15 different tab settings across one line. This command is often used in conjunction with the C command. The prestored tabs are only usable in the insert mode, using the command 'I'

TB 1 10 20 30

Will set tabs at columns 1, 10, 20 and 30. This is particularly useful when updating screen layouts in a PROC.

U - Up.   This command moves the current line pointer back by the number of specified lines.

X-Delete effect   The effect of the last Input, Insert, Delete or Replace is nullified. This is seen in Figure 9.21, when a replace statement has been wrongly entered. The delete effect will not work if an 'F' (File) command has taken place.

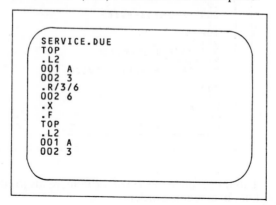

```
SERVICE.DUE
TOP
.L2
001  A
002  3
.R/3/6
002  6
.X
.F
TOP
.L2
001  A
002  3
```

Figure 9.21

132

Chapter 10

The BASIC Language

"A language is a system of signs or symbols used for conveying information."
Oxford English Dictionary.

Introduction

The Pick operating system includes a BASIC language processor as a general purpose programming tool. The Pick operating system BASIC is an extended version of standard Dartmouth BASIC, the very popular programming language. Since most computer professionals are at least acquainted with BASIC, and many documents discuss the features of this versatile language, this section will cover only those features of the Pick operating system BASIC that are specifically unique, or are otherwise standard functions that strongly interact with other Pick operating system unique software or hardware.

The History of BASIC

The BASIC language was developed in 1965 by John G Kemey and Thomas E Kurtz of Dartmouth College USA, primarily as a language for introductory courses in computer science for non science students. BASIC is one of a number of high level languages. These languages fall into one of two categories, general purpose and specific. FORTRAN (Formula Translation) was specifically designed for scientific number crunching tasks and is used extensively in scientific research; while COBOL (Common Business Orientated Language) is for business and information retrieval purposes. General purpose languages include:

> PL/1
> ADA
> ALGOL 68

Since its conception BASIC has fallen from favour in the academic world, but has become popular in other spheres. The objective of BASIC was for it to be easy to use and learn, which has resulted in a simply yet versatile programming language suitable for expressing a wide range of problems.

Why BASIC?

When the Pick operating system was first designed, BASIC was the only high level language that was both suitable and available for use. Richard Pick, the designer of the operating system named after him, originally wanted to use APL (Advanced Programming Language), which is a more theoretical than practical language. Some people are put off BASIC by the reputation it has earned as a home computer buff's language, and it tends not to be taken seriously by professionals, as they believe it to be too elementary. But, Pick BASIC is different. It has the ability to write structured code, to talk and communicate with peripherals such as a tape deck, and to chain subroutines together, as well as sophisticated file handling facilities. Admittedly, the Pick operating system is tied to a single language, but that language is fully integrated with all the other parts of the system. By being so tightly integrated, BASIC can use the system's other facilities to full advantage from within any program. This gives advance knowledge to the programmer of any Pick machine, what the data structures are and how they are handled by DATA/BASIC.

By using a high level language, total machine independence can and should be achieved. This is found to be the case on any Pick machine. A program developed on one Pick machine will run on another. This is a great advantage over a traditional computing environment where there are as many variations in the BASIC language as there are in regional dialects in the English language. This is because there has been no industry standard, an each manufacturer has put in their own slight, but annoying, modifications. Annoying that is for a programmer, and annoying for a business man with PC DOS and CP/M who will need two different versions of a single package just to accommodate the different versions of BASIC. Perhaps the biggest reason for the Pick system to be tied to one language is standardisation. In advance of using any Pick machine, the programmer is aware of how Pick BASIC integrates with the other parts of the system and what, therefore, can be achieved. Pick BASIC also gives the following advantages:

1. More convenient descriptions of the tasks which are to be performed.

2. More efficient program writing with less time spent debugging the program and more time solving the problem in hand.

3. More productivity. High level languages make programs easier and faster to write! about ten times faster than using assembly code.

4. Easier documentation. As the code is more readable, some simple programs can be almost self-documenting. This means that programs now need very little effort to achieve traditional longhand documentation.

5. Standard syntax. Most high level languages have ani nternational set of standards, setting out the meaning and functionality of each 'word'.

Additional words are often added by individual manufacturers; in the Pick world the Ultimate range of computers has enhanced Pick BASIC.

6. Portabilty. As long as the same version of the compiler and the same or standard syntax is used, the code will be portable to other machines using the same combination.

Re-entrant Code.

The BASIC processor generates re-entrant codes which can be shared among a number of users. In practice, this means that if a program is used by a number of users simultaneously, only one copy of the program needs to be present in memory.

Source Files

Pick BASIC source files, like all files on the system, consist of a number of items. Each program is an item in a file. The typical user will have one file for all programs and each item will contain one program. The item identifier is the name of the program and each complete line of the program is an attribute.

Interpreters and compilers

BASIC, being a high level language, needs to be translated into a form that the computer will understand. There are two processes of translation, one is interpretation, the other is compilation. Interpretation and compilation are two entirely different approaches to obtaining the human type input in machine format, which in turn allows the program to be executed.

An interpreter does not generate a complete set of object code for a program. As each source statement is looked at by the interpreter, it is immediately analysed followed by execution. If one statement is found to be incorrect the interpreter will stop there and issue a pertinent error message. If there are many errors it can take some time to correct all the mistakes one by one, whereas with a compiler all the mistakes are listed in one go and need to be corrected before execution can be repeated. The interpretation technique is represented in Figure 10.1. The major advantage of an interpreter is that it offers an easier, more gentle, learning curve for the first time programmer. With an interpreter there is no need to learn about the process of compiling and syntax is checked automatically for each statement.

A simple compiler translates the input text (known as the source code) into an equivalent machine code, leaving two versions of the program. The first is the source code and the second, unreadable machine code, (known as object code). This is seen in Figure 10.2. The translation process takes place

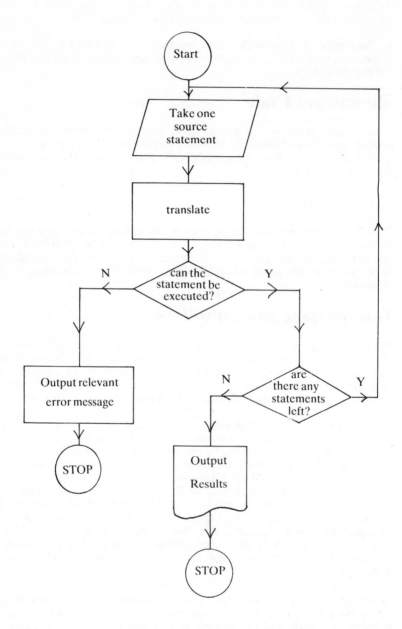

Figure 10.1

on all of the source code, in one fell swoop. It is the object code that the operating system actually uses in order to execute or run a program, but, take the source file away, leaving just the object code and the program will still be able to continue running as if nothing had happened. Many software packages deliberately carry only the object code. By removing the source code the program becomes protected, first from the software pirate and secondly from unauthorised alteration of the program, thereby making a standard piece of software nonstandard.

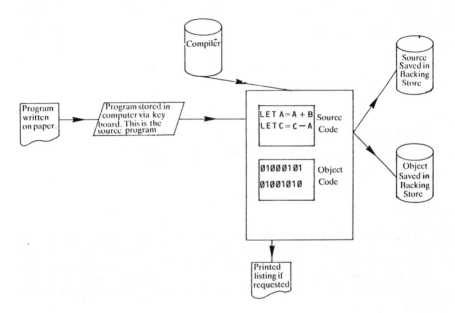

Figure 10.2A compiler reads the high level source statements and translates them into machine code, which is stored for future use.

Pick uses the compilation method of translation mainly because compilation has the advantage of speed. Even when the program is functioning perfectly, an interpreter still carries on checking each and every line, so the interpreted language is almost inevitably slower. The compilation process is more suited to the multi-user environment for which all Pick machines are designed.

The object code that is produced by Pick BASIC is written to disk, and a special pointer is then written to the dictionary of the source file. This pointer contains the location of the object code on disk, this is shown in Figure 10.3.

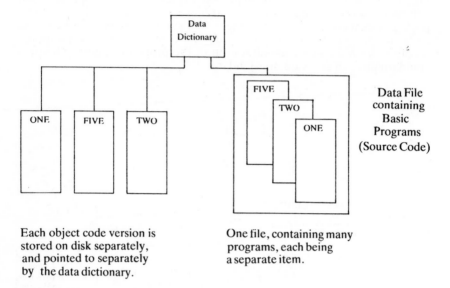

Each object code version is stored on disk separately, and pointed to separately by the data dictionary.	One file, containing many programs, each being a separate item.

Figure 10.3

As Figure 10.3 shows, each object code module is stored independently in a contiguous segment of one or more frames on disk, while the source code is stored as an item in one file. Both are tracked by one dictionary. The compiler creates the pointer for each object module in the file dictionary associated with the source, automatically creating a new unique dictionary item.

This special file definition item, has special functions for each attribute:

Attribute 1 This contains "CC", indicating this item points to compiled object code.

Attribute 2 This is the number of the first frame of compiled code, used for locating the program at run time.

Attribute 3 This contains a number, giving the total number of frames that the compiled code occupies.

Attribute 4 This attribute is always left null.

Attribute 5 This contains the data and time (taken from the system) of the last compilation process this program went through.

138

Features of the Pick BASIC compiler.

The compiler includes a number of options to assist the programmer in the development and debugging of BASIC programs. All options that produce listings are optionally available at the line printer rather than at the terminal.

1. A line by line list of the program, as it is compiled, complete with error messages 2. A list of the numbers of the lines in which each of the variables appear. This information is stored on a file and can be looked at via the Access processor, providing a special item called BSYM has been defined in the user's master dictionary. The statement:

```
SORT BSYM BY LINE-NUMBER LINE-NUMBER
```
will generate a print-out from the file of stored information. The file is cleared before each compilation which uses this facility. 3. The ability to list only the errors and the line on which they appear.

Executing BASIC programs.

Once a BASIC program has been compiled, it can be run by using the RUN command followed by the name of the dictionary containing the file definition item pointing to the object code.

The CATALOG command will create a pointer to the object code in the Master dictionary of the user concerned. This allows the BASIC program to be invoked via a verb at TCL level. This is achieved by using the statement:

```
CATALOG BP EXAMPLE
```

at TCL. Where BP is the filename and EXAMPLE the item identifier, this causes an item to be entered in the user's master dictionary. Once the program is catalogued, it is executed by simply entering the program name at TCL. From the users point of view, the program has become a system command or 'verb', like any other.

File handling in BASIC

Traditionally, file handling in BASIC has been virtually non existent, but the Pick operating system BASIC has been enhanced to provide a number of unique features for file handling. These take advantage of the database management functions in the operating system's file manager. The BASIC programmer using the Pick Operating system has a set of already developed, application independent, data management tools that can significantly reduce development time.

The chapter on file structure discusses the operating system's management of disk files, but in summary:

1. A Pick operating system file contains one or more items. These items are identified by an item identifier. Items contain one or more attributes and an attribute can contain one or more values. Finally, values can contain one or more subvalues. Attributes, values and subvalues are all delimited by special markers.

2. An item is a string consisting of combinations of these elements and can be up to 32K bytes in length. In Pick BASIC, this string can be loaded into a dynamically dimension array.

Dynamic Array handling Functions

A dynamic array is data held in the same format as a file item, i.e. any number of attributes separated by special markers. A dynamic array has a single variable name, individual elements of the array being referenced by special Pick BASIC functions, provided for the purpose. There are also statements for reading and writing an item from backing store into a dynamic array and vice versa. Once an item has been loaded into a dynamic array, there are various functions for extracting the contents of a specific attribute, value, or subvalue; replacing attributes, values and subvalues, and counting the numbers of attributes within an item. These features are particularly powerful when used to read and write items directly to or from a disk.

For example the following data item:

```
    WHITE LION
001 01-456-7799
002 TONIC]DRY GINGER]BITTER LEMON
003 30
004 12
005 MARK PRIOR
006 10 THE DRIVE CRICKLEWOOD
```

can be read from disk by using the statement:

```
READ EXAMPLE FORM CUSTOMER, 'WHITE LION' ELSE STOP
```

After the execution of this statement the variable EXAMPLE will contain the dynamic array value

```
01-456-7799^TONIC]DRY GINGER]BITTER
LEMON^30^12^MARK PRIOR^10 THE DRIVE
CRICKLEWOOD
```

The form of the data storage is known as 'item-format'. The term dynamic is used because the shape and size of the array is not fixed, and may be altered freely by other statements and functions in the rest of the program.

These dynamic arrays interface well with the file item, as an entire item can be read or written and individual values can be easily accessed. The dimensioned arrays are more advantageous when a large number of elements are being accessed or if processing large items as each field is placed in a separate variable location.

Once an item has been loaded into a dynamic array the EXTRACT function can return the contents of a specific attribute, value or subvalue. The EXTRACT function then specifies the dynamic array, the attribute number, the value number and the subvalue number to be extracted. For instance:

```
OPEN '','EXAMPLE' TO TEMP ELSE STOP
READ ITEM FROM 'TEMP', 'WHITE LION' ELSE STOP
X = EXTRACT (ITEM,2,2,0)
```

The first parameter in the function gives the name of the dynamic array that is going to have data extracted. The second parameter gives the attribute, the third the number of a value in the attribute (a multivalue) and the forth a subvalue. The above command will extract the second value of the second attribute in the specified array. The extracted value of DRY GINGER is then assigned to variable X.

The REPLACE function provides the corresponding capability to change the value of the contents of a value in the array. For instance, DRY GINGER could be replaced by PINEAPPLE JUICE using the following sequence of statements:

```
OPEN '', 'EXAMPLE' TO TEMP ELSE STOP
READ ITEM FROM 'TEMP' , 'WHITE LION' ELSE STOP
ITEM  =  REPLACE(ITEM,2,2,0;'PINEAPPLE  JUICE')
WRITE ITEM ON 'EXAMPLE'
```

The item WHITE LION has been read from the database and placed in the dynamic array ITEM. The second value of the second attribute is then replaced, and written back to the file EXAMPLE.

DELETE allows for deletion of a specific attribute, value or subvalue. INSERT allows the insertion of a new attribute, value or subvalue. A more detailed description can be found in Appendix D.

The LOCATE statement is used to find a specified value (if present) in a dynamic array. The statement would be used for the location and/or insertion of controlling and dependant attributes within the dictionary items. For instance:

```
LOCATE('D',ITEM,4;VAR) ELSE ITEM = INSERT (ITEM,4,VAR,0,'D')
```

the fourth attribute of the dynamic array ITEM is searched for the alphabetic literal 'D' and the location of the array when the literal is found is placed in the variable VAR. If the 'D' is not found the location of the beginning of the fourth attribute is returned in VAR giving the position where 'D' should be. If it is not found, control is passed to the ELSE clause, which will insert the missing 'D' in the correct place, by using the "should be here" marker in VAR. This single statement can often eliminate the need for a loop, which may have had to specifically extract and test the attribute and provide alternative routes before the next item could be searched.

The COUNT function will count the number of occurrences of a specified string within attributes, values or subvalues of an item.

Using these functions, the full range of database facilities available on the Pick operating system are also available to the BASIC programmer. Not only simplifying the BASIC program itself, but ensuring compatibility with the Access Processor, for reporting at a later date.

Other features.

The MATCH statement provides pattern matching facilities in BASIC similar to those available in the PROC processor. These include testing for a number of alpha or numeric characters and literal string comparison.

The CHAIN function will transfer control to another BASIC program or any valid TCL command including a PROC. Variables can be passed to the chained program.

The PRINTER ON, PRINTER OFF, and PRINTER CLOSE statements cause output to be directed to the spooler or the user's terminal. When the program is finished, the spooled file will become eligible for printing. If spooling prior to the end of the program is desired, the PRINTER CLOSE statement will immediately spool the accumulated output.

Output functions, similar to the modifier functions found in the Access query language, include justification, both left and right, specification of the number of digits to the right of the decimal point, descaling of numbers, the suppression of leading zeros,the insertion of commas, printing of "DB" or the minus sign after negative numbers, printing "CR" after positive numbers, appending currency signs to numbers, and filling a predetermined length field with any specified character.

The HEADING and FOOTING functions, similar to the same functions in the Access query language, help output pages to be formatted when output is being prepared for reports. A heading or footing is stored using the relevant BASIC function, and is actually actioned by the use of the PAGE statement in a program. PAGE also accepts a variable from the program as a parameter, to set a page number counter. Optional parameters for the

HEADING and FOOTING functions will automatically incorporate the time and date, assign page numbers, centre text, and insert blank lines.

The PROMPT statement selects a character to be printed at the user's terminal whenever the program stops for input. (Usually when the INPUT statement is used). For example:

PROMPT "+"

will cause a 'plus sign' to be displayed as the prompt character at the user's terminal.

The READNEXT statement reads a list of item ids from a list supplied by the Access processor SELECT or SSELECT. These items can then be brought into a dynamic array for processing. READNEXT statements can continue until the list is exhausted.

BASIC also has access to the magnetic tape or floppy disk unit by the use of READT, WRITET, WEOF) write end of file mark) and REWIND statements.

Multi-User File Locks

If one or more BASIC programs are running concurrently, and they access the same file, multi user lock-out protection is necessary in order to prevent the two programs from writing to the same data without co-ordination. Even a simple accounting system cannot allow two clerks to run the same ledger program at the same time unless this protection is available. This problem is somewhat compounded in a database oriented system, since an attribute like ACCOUNT NUMBER might exist in only one file, but be accessed by several programs. Without file lockout protection, the entire accounting system might be accessible to only one user at a time. The Pick operating system BASIC offers a sophisticated set of locks to co-ordinate multiple user access to the same files.

File locking is implemented with modified versions of the READ and WRITE statements. When one of these modified statements is executed, the group (defined in the modulo and separation of the file concerned) in which the read takes place is "locked" or placed out of bounds, to other programs until released by the locking program.

For the most part, a group is a user transparent concept. It is, however, the fundamental block of data which the Pick operating system uses internally for reading and writing. Since a group is a subset of an entire file, two users will still be able to access the file at the same time; they just can't access items in the same group at the same time.

If a program attempts to read data from, or write data to, a group that is locked by another program, the program will wait until the group becomes unlocked. Use of conditional parameters with modified READ and WRITE statements can be used to gracefully branch to another part of the program to deal with a lockout situation. The RELEASE statement unlocks groups, and all locked groups locked by a specific BASIC program are unlocked when that program ends. The Pick operating system can keep track of up to 62 locked groups at a time.

Structured Programming

Unlike most other versions of BASIC, the Pick BASIC contains all the commands that are needed to write structured code. One of the complaints from academics about BASIC has been its unstructured form. The term 'structure' is one of those words which tend to occur in conversation between programmers. It refers to a set of rules and regulations set down by a collection of influential high level language writers. The term structure also comes in useful for consultants and those well versed in criticism, in that a program which works well and is quite acceptable can be condemned for 'poor structure'. A well structured language means it is easy to design and follow the solution to a problem, and the code of such a solution does not end up resembling a pile of spaghetti (one big muddle)! Structured programs in ordinary BASIC are somewhat difficult to write, but the modifications carried out on Pick BASIC have made structuring a lot easier. It is very easy when programming in any BASIC to build up a program without giving much thought to its overall structure. The fact that rigid restrictions are not imposed upon the programmer allows the program to be tested and amended over and over again. While a program is under development this can be both a blessing and a curse. It is a blessing when offering freedom and flexibility, but a curse when giving a muddled appearance. Lack of structure makes error finding and correction a nightmare, therefore Pick BASIC contains all the constraints needed to write highly structured code. Among the commands available are:

```
CASE
COMMON
IF...THEN....ELSE
FOR....NEXT
FOR....UNTIL
FOR....WHILE
LOOP....WHILE
LOOP....UNTIL
```

These are all fully explained in Appendix D.

144

Summary

One of Pick's strong points is that it makes applications easy to write. Many time consuming chores that are found in other languages, such as writing complex input output routines and complex data file manipulations, are either not necessary with Pick or can be done with existing system utilities in another part of the operating system but integrated allowing use. In addition Pick BASIC has a powerful facility to automatically generate a program map and variable cross reference tables upon compilation of the program.

The BASIC language as implemented on the PICK machines is a simple programming language enabling easy manipulation of numbers and character strings. That is why it is particularly suitable as a language for implementing management/database applications. It is particularly easy for the beginner to master. This was one of the primary objectives when it was first written. BASIC programs can be stored, compiled, tested and executed on the system through any terminal, at the same time other users may develop programs or execute existing programs, thus giving total interactive computing.

BASIC operates on variables of any length, type or number. It can call on subroutine sequences or on system utilities, enabling control as well as efficient organisation of data allowing straight forward interrogation via screens or printers.

The processes which are included in the Pick operating system include a compiler, a syntax checker, error analyser, a number of diagnosis and test utilities, and a trace function which enables the monitoring of program execution. The constraints of a multiprocessing environment are resolved through the use of locks and individual work-files.

The Pick BASIC language was specifically designed with PICK in mind and features:

1. A set of file access and update statements.

2. String and file processing items.

3. A clear language structure allowing structured programming.

4. Error finding aids.

5. Access to magnetic tape commands.

6. Ability to integrate external subroutines.

The BASIC processor complements the Pick operating system with this popular procedural programming language. Since the full range of data base management functions are available to the BASIC programmer, as implemented in the Access processor, the complementary combination of capabilities of these two processors can be used to bring new applications on-line faster than would be the case using conventional file structures and totally procedural languages.

Chapter 11

Runoff

This chapter deals with "Runoff" - that part of the Pick operating system designed to help with the production of the inevitable manual which accompanies each and every piece of software. Runoff was originally a simple word processor, but the advances in the quality and facilities offered by word processing packages has pushed runoff into insignificance and to being classified as a text processor.

A runoff document has two parts. First, the actual text of the document and, secondly, the commands to format that text as required. These formatting commands take the form of "dot commands" similar to those found in Wordstar, a popular word processor for microcomputers.

As in all other parts of the Pick operating system, each document is held in an item in a file, shown in Figure 11.1.

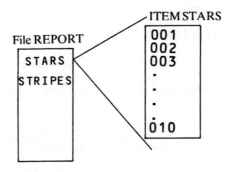

Figure 11.1

Runoff will number pages automatically, print text headers and footers, perform tabulations, centre a piece of text and select right or left justification at a tabulation stop. And, when writing an entire publication, the indexing may be done at the press of a button.

Shown below is a basic example of a runoff item:

```
     STARS
001  .BP
002  .LINE LENGTH 55
003  .J
004  .PARAGRAPH 4
005  Aquarius....... A bright future ahead, with an expansion of
     ambitions, and plenty of social opportunities. You'll be
     fairly unruffled by today's
006  restless conditions.
007  .BREAK
008  Pisces.........Neptune, your ruler, is strongly aspected
009  raising controversy in financial affairs.
010  Make time for checking accounts.
011  .BREAK
012  Aries.......... An edgy phase if you are relying on the co-
     operation of companions.
013  Goods and services might not come up to scratch.
014  .BREAK
015  Taurus......... Not easy to feel enthusiastic about
016  routine chores, so aim for variation and get out and about a
     bit.
017  Fresh senses will spark off new ideas.
018  .BREAK
019  Gemini......... Group activities need organising if you don't
     want to run round in circles
020  and then find yourself out of pocket.
```

The above example shows a source document complete with all the formatting commands such as:

.BREAK   Start a new line
.BP   Begin a new page

On issuing the command:

RUNOFF REPORT STARS

which consists of the command RUNOFF, the file name and the item name held within that file, the source document is fed into the processor and the formatting commands applied to the text giving the output:

```
Aquarius....... A bright future ahead, with an expansion of
ambitions, and plenty of social opportunities. You'll be
fairly unruffled by today's restless conditions.
Pisces......... Neptune, your ruler, is strongly aspected
raising controversy in financial affairs. Make time for
checking accounts.
Aries.......... An edgy phase if you are relying on the co-
operation of companions. Goods and services might not come up
to scratch.
Taurus......... Not easy to feel enthusiastic about routine
chores, so aim for variation and get out and about a bit. Fresh
senses will spark off new ideas.
Gemini......... Group activities need organising if you
don't want to run round in circles. And then find yourself out of
pocket.
```

Each line in the file is treated as a straightforward and simple output of text, unless the first character on the line is a full stop (period). The command lines, as they are known, may contain more than one formatter. For example the first few lines of the example can be reduced to one line as shown.

```
      STARS
001  .BP.LINE LENGTH 55.J.PARAGRAPH 4
002  Aquarius.......A bright future ahead, with
     an expansion of ambitions, and plenty of      social opportunities.
You'll be
```

This will give exactly the same output as shown above, but puts all the formatting commands in one place.

Each of the runoff commands are listed below, showing their effect on the document called STARS. As many or as few of these commands as are needed can be used in a single document.

. *

Any text that follows the . * tells the runoff processor that a comment is about to follow. This allows the purpose of the document to be explained in the item. This facility can be very useful particularly if each document has the first line as a descriptive comment. A dictionary item can then be set up and used via the Access language to obtain a description of each of the runoff items in a particular file.

For example:

```
      STARS
001  .* TODAY'S HORROR SCOPE !!
002  .BP.LINE LENGTH 55.J.PARAGRAPH 4
003  Aquarius.......A bright future ahead, with
     an expansion of ambitions, and plenty of
     social opportunities. You'll be fairly
     unruffled by today's
004  restless conditions.
```

In the dictionary of the file REPORT the following item is present:

```
            DESCRIPTION
      001 A
      002 1
      003 DESCRIPTION
      004
      005
      006
      007
      008
      009 L
      010 35
```

When an Access command using the dictionary item DESCRIPTION is
used, the first attribute of each item in the REPORT file is output as a piece
of data, allowing a list of names and descriptions of each report to be output.
The following command

LIST REPORT DESCRIPTION

gives the output:

```
PAGE   1                        13:00:00   24 JAN 1985

REPORT....DESCRIPTION...........................
STARS      TODAY'S HORROR SCOPE !!

1 ITEMS LISTED.
```

.BP or .BEGIN PAGE

The textual output is halted, and the screen or the printer advances to the
top of the next page, giving output as seen in Figure 11.2.

```
      STARS
001 .*-TODAY+S HORROR SCOPE !!
002 .BP.LINE LENGTH 55.J.PARAGRAPH 4
003 Aquarius....... A bright future ahead, with an expansion of
    ambitions, and plenty of social opportunities. You'll be
    fairly unruffled by today's
004 restless conditions.
005 .BP
006 Pisces........Neptune, your ruler, is strongly aspected
007 raising controversy in financial affairs.
008 Make time for checking accounts.
009 .BP
010 Aries.......... An edgy phase if you are relying on the co-
    operation of companions.
011 Goods and services might not come up to scratch.
012 .BP
013 Taurus......... Not easy to feel enthusiastic about
014 routine chores, so aim for variation and get out and about
    a bit.
015 Fresh senses will spark off new ideas.
016 .BP
017 Gemini......... Group activities need organising if you
    don't want to run round in circles
018 and then find yourself out of pocket.
```

150

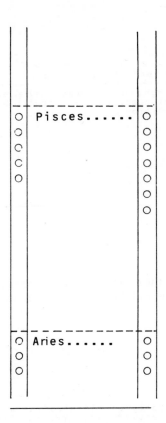

Figure 11.2

.BOX

This is a graphic presentation device, which encloses a piece of text in a box. This command works with an on/off switch. The first **.BOX** command switches the facility on, the second switches it off.

```
        STARS
001 .* TODAY'S HORROR SCOPE !!
002 .BP.LINE LENGTH 55.J.PARAGRAPH 4
003 .BOX 6,55.CENTER
004 The Horror Scope for Today
005 .BOX
006 Aquarius....... A bright future ahead, with
    an expansion of ambitions, and plenty of
    social opportunities. You'll be
```

Which gives :

```
-----------------------------------------------------
  :          The Horror Scope for Today         :
-----------------------------------------------------
Aquarius....... A bright future ahead, with an expansion of ambitions,
and plenty of social opportunities. You'll be fairly unruffled by
today's restless conditions.
```

BREAK

This command causes the previous line not to be right justified. The next line of text starts on a new line at the left margin. This can be seen in the example:

```
      STARS
001   .BP
002   .LINE LENGTH 55
003   .J
004   .PARAGRAPH 4
005   Aquarius...... A bright future ahead, with an expansion of
      ambitions, and plenty of social opportunities. You'll be
      fairly unruffled by today's
006   restless conditions.
007   .BREAK
008   Pisces....... Neptune, your ruler, is strongly aspected
009   raising controversy in financial affairs.
010   Make time for checking accounts.
011   .BREAK
012   Aries.......... An edgy phase if you are relying on the co-
      operation of companions.
013   Goods and services might not come up to scratch.
014   .BREAK
015   Taurus......... Not easy to feel enthusiastic about
016   routine chores, so aim for variation and get out and about
      a bit.
017   Fresh senses will spark off new ideas.
018   .BREAK
019   Gemini......... Group activities need organising if you
      don't want to run round in circles
020   and then find yourself out of pocket.
```

Giving:

```
Aquarius....... A bright future ahead, with an expansion of
ambitions, and plenty of social opportunities. You'll be
fairly unruffled by today's restless conditions.
Pisces......... Neptune, your ruler, is strongly aspected
raising controversy in financial affairs. Make time for
checking accounts.
Aries.......... An edgy phase if you are relying on the co-
operation of companions. Goods and services might not come up
to scratch.
Taurus......... Not easy to feel enthusiastic about routine
chores, so aim for variation and get out and senses will spark
off new ideas.
Gemini......... Group activities need organising if you don't
want to run round in circles. And then find yourself out of
pocket.
```

.CENTER

This command retains the American spelling. The line of text following this
command is placed in the centre of the page.

Example:

```
        STARS
001  .* TODAY'S HORROR SCOPE !!
002  .BP.LINE LENGTH 55.J.PARAGRAPH 4
003  .BOX 6,55.CENTER
004  The Horror Scope for Today
005  .BOX
006  Aquarius....... A bright future ahead, with an expansion of
        ambitions, and plenty of social opportunities. You'll be
        fairly unruffled by today's
007  .CENTER
008  restless conditions.
009  .BREAK
010  Pisces......... Neptune, your ruler, is
        strongly aspected
011  raising controversy in finacial affairs.
```

Giving:

```
----------------------------------------------------
:            The Horror Scope for Today          :
----------------------------------------------------
Aquarius........A bright future ahead, with an
expansion of ambitions, and plenty of social
opportunities. You'll be fairly unruffled by today's
                   restless conditions.
Pisces.........Neptune, your ruler, is strongly
aspected raising controversy in financial affairs.
```

.CHAIN

This command allows a document to be output any number of times, inserting information from different items in a data file. This is used in conjunction with **.READNEXT**, and a full example is found in the **.READNEXT** section.

.CHAPTER

A useful facility for any budding author. This command automatically numbers chapters and puts a textual heading.

For example:

```
     STARS
001  .* TODAY'S HORROR SCOPE !!
002  .BP.LINE LENGTH 55.J.PARAGRAPH 4
003  .CENTER
004  .CHAPTER THE DAILY PREDICTIONS
005  .BOX 6,55.CENTER
006  The Horror Scope for Today
007  .BOX
008  Aquarius........A bright future ahead, with
     an expansion of
     ambitions, and plenty of social
     opportunities. You'll be fairly unruffled by
     today's
009  restless conditions.
```

Giving:

CHAPTER 1

THE DAILY PREDICTIONS

```
---------------------------------------------------
:               The Horror Scope for Today         :
---------------------------------------------------
Aquarius........A bright future ahead, with an
expansion of ambitions, and plenty of social
opportunities. You'll be fairly unruffled by today's
restless conditions.
Pisces.........Neptune, your ruler, is strongly
```

In this example there is only one chapter, but subsequent chapter commands in the same document will cause the chapter number to be incremented.

.CONTENTS

This command will print a table of contents from accumulated information from .CHAPTER and .SECTION commands. This should only be used at the end of a runoff document.

```
    STARS
001 .* TODAY'S HORROR SCOPE !!
002 .BP.LINE LENGTH 55.J.PARAGRAPH 4
003 .CENTER
004 .CHAPTER THE DAILY PREDICTIONS
005 .BOX 6,55.CENTER
006 The Horror Scope for Today
007 .BOX
008 Aquarius.......A bright future ahead, with an expansion
    of ambitions, and plenty of social opportunities. You'll
    be fairly unruffled by today's
009 restless conditions.
010 .BREAK
011 Pisces.........Neptune, your ruler, is strongly
    aspected
012 raising controversy in financial affairs.
013 Make time for checking accounts.
014 .BREAK
015 Aries..........An edgy phase if you are relying on the co-
    operation of companions.
016 Goods and services might not come up to scratch.
017 .BREAK
018 Taurus.........Not easy to feel enthusiastic about
019 routine chores, so aim for variation and get out and about a
    bit.
020 Fresh senses will spark off new ideas.
021 .BREAK
022 Gemini.........Group activities need organising if you
    don't want to run round in circles
023 and then find yourself out of pocket.
024 .CONTENTS
```

Giving:

```
                            CHAPTER 1

                      THE DAILY PREDICTIONS

          ---------------------------------------------------
          :                The Horror Scope for Today         :
          ---------------------------------------------------
        Aquarius........ A bright future ahead, with an
        expansion of ambitions, and plenty of social
        opportunities. You'll be fairly unruffled by today's
        restless conditions.
        Pisces......... Neptune, your ruler, is strongly
        aspected raising controversy in financial affairs.
        Make time for checking accounts.
        Aries.......... An edgy phase if you are relying on
        the co-operation of companions. Goods and services
        might not come up to scratch.
        Taurus......... Not easy to feel enthusiastic about
        routine chores, so aim for variation and get out and
        about a bit. Fresh senses will spark off new ideas.
        Gemini......... Group activities need organising if you
        don't want to run round in circles. And then find
        yourself out of pocket.

        ------------------------------------------------(New page)
                         TABLE OF CONTENTS
        SECTION                                            PAGE
        1           THE DAILY PREDICTIONS . . . . . . . . .   1
                         _____
```

.FILL

This command means that each line that is output is automatically filled to capacity, without overflowing. If justification mode is switched on, runoff will insert spaces in the line at random to make the right hand margin line up. .FILL is a standard setting.

.FOOTING

This command prints the next line of text as a footer to each page. For example:

```
STARS
001 .* TODAY'S HORROR SCOPE !!
002 .BP.LINE LENGTH 55.J.PARAGRAPH 4
003 .FOOTING
004 Sponsored by THE STAR AT NIGHT
005 .CENTER
006 .CHAPTER THE DAILY PREDICTIONS
007 .BOX 6,55.CENTER
008 The Horror Scope for Today 009 .BOX
010 Aquarius....... A bright future ahead, with an expansion
    of ambitions, and plenty of social opportunities. You'll
    be fairly unruffled by today's
```

Giving the output shown in Figure 11.3.

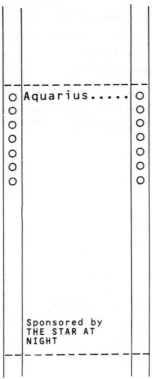

Figure 11.3

.HEADING

The same function as footing except that the text is output at the top of each new page. As in the **.FOOTING** command, the text is output from the left margin. No centering will automatically take place. Top get the heading centred, use:

.CENTER.HEADING

Giving the following item, and output as in figure 11.4

```
      STARS
001  .* TODAY'S HORROR SCOPE !!
002  .BP.LINE LENGTH 55.J.PARAGRAPH 4
003  .CENTER.HEADING
004  This is brought to you using the latest technology
005  .FOOTING
006  Sponsored by THE STAR AT NIGHT
007  .CENTER
008  .CHAPTER THE DAILY PREDICTIONS
009  .BOX 6,55.CENTER
010  The Horror Scope for Today
011  .BOX
012  Aquarius........ A bright future ahead, with an expansion
     of ambitions, and plenty of social opportunities. You'll
     be fairly unruffled by today's
```

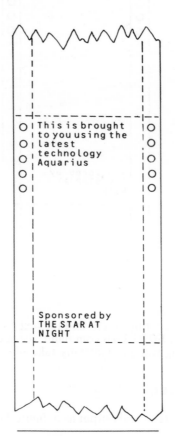

Figure 11.4

.INDENT

The next line of text will be indented by the required number of column positions from the left margin, which in our case is presently set to zero.

```
      STARS
001 .* TODAY'S HORROR SCOPE !!
002 .BP.LINE LENGTH 55.J.PARAGRAPH 4
003 .CENTER
004 .CHAPTER THE DAILY PREDICTIONS
005 .BOX 6,55.CENTER
006 The Horror Scope for Today
007 .BOX
008 Aquarius....... A bright future ahead, with an expansion
    of ambitions, and plenty of social opportunities. You'll
    be fairly unruffled by today's
009 restless conditions.
010 .BREAK
011 Pisces......... Neptune, your ruler, is strongly aspected
012 raising controversy in financial affairs.
013 Make time for checking accounts.
014 .BREAK
015 Aries.......... An edgy phase if you are relying on the co-
    operation of companions.
016 Goods and services might not come up to scratch.
017 .BREAK
018 Taurus......... Not easy to feel enthusiastic about
019 .INDENT 5
020 routine chores, so aim for variation and get out and about a
    bit.
021 .INDENT 10
022 Fresh senses will spark off new ideas.
023 .BREAK
024 Gemini......... Group activities need organising if you
    don't want to run round in circles
025 and then find yourself out of pocket.
```

Giving:

CHAPTER 1

THE DAILY PREDICTIONS

```
---------------------------------------------------
:  _____The Horror Scope for Today_____ :
---------------------------------------------------
Aquarius....... A bright future ahead, with an
expansion of ambitions, and plenty of social
opportunities. You'll be fairly unruffled by today's
restless conditions.
Pisces......... Neptune, your ruler, is strongly
aspected raising controversy in financial affairs.
Make time for checking accounts.
Aries.......... An edgy phase if you are relying on
the co-operation of companions. Goods and services
might not come up to scratch.
Taurus......... Not easy to feel enthusiastic about
     routine chores, so aim for variation and get out and
about a bit.
          Fresh senses will spark off new ideas.
Gemini......... Group activities need organising if you
don't want to run round in circles. And then find
yourself out of pocket.
```

.IM n or .INDENT MARGIN n

The width of the left margin is increased by the given number, and the length of the line decreased by the same amount.

```
      STARS 001 .* TODAY'S HORROR SCOPE !!
002   .BP .LINE LENGTH 55 .J .PARAGRAPH 4
003   .CENTER
004   .CHAPTER THE DAILY PREDICTIONS
005   .BOX 6,55 .CENTER
006   The Horror Scope for Today
007   .BOX
008   Aquarius....... A bright future ahead, with an expansion
      of ambitions, and plenty of social opportunities. You'll
      be fairly unruffled by today's
009   restless conditions.
010   .BREAK
011   Pisces......... Neptune, your ruler, is strongly
      aspected
012   raising controversy in financial affairs.
013   Make time for checking accounts.
014   .BREAK
015   Aries.......... An edgy phase if you are relying on the
      co-operation of companions.
016   Goods and services might not come up to scratch.
017   .BREAK
018   Taurus......... Not easy to feel enthusiastic about
019   .INDENT MARGIN 5
020   routine chores, so aim for variation and get out and about a
      bit.
021   .INDENT MARGIN 15
022   Fresh senses will spark off new ideas.
023   .BREAK
024   Gemini......... Group activities need organising if you
      don+t want to run round in circles
025   and then find yourself out of pocket.
```

Giving:

CHAPTER 1

THE DAILY PREDICTIONS

```
-------------------------------------------------
:            The Horror Scope for Today          :
-------------------------------------------------
```

Aquarius....... A bright future ahead, with an
expansion of ambitions, and plenty of social
opportunities. You'll be fairly unruffled by today+s
restless conditions.
Pisces......... Neptune, your ruler, is strongly
aspected raising controversy in financial affairs.
Make time for checking accounts.
Aries.......... An edgy phase if you are relying on
the co-operation of companions. Goods and services
might not come up to scratch.
Taurus......... Not easy to feel enthusiastic about
      routine chores, so aim for variation and get out
      and about a bit.
                  Fresh senses will spark off new ideas.
                  Gemini......... Group activities need
                  organising if you don't want to run
                  round in circles. And then find
                  yourself out of pocket.

```
```

As can be seen the new margin applies to any following text, until the next margin statement is applied.

.INDEX

This again is helpful when compiling a large document which requires an index. Just type **.INDEX** and the term required:

.INDEX Aquarius

Then, the page number(s) where that word appears is/are stored, and subsequently listed by using the **.PRINT INDEX** command.

.INPUT

This command allows runoff to take text from the user's terminal rather than from the current file item. A prompt is output to the terminal, and the reply is inserted into the item without causing a break to occur.

Consider the following example:

```
     STARS
001  .* TODAY'S HORROR SCOPE !!
002  .BP.LINE LENGTH 55 .J.PARAGRAPH 4
003  .CENTER
004  .CHAPTER THE DAILY PREDICTIONS
005  .BOX 6,55.CENTER
006  The Horror Scope for Today
007  .BOX
008  Aquarius....... A bright future ahead, with an expansion
     of
     ambitions, and plenty of social opportunities. You'll be
     fairly unruffled by today's
009  restless conditions.
010  .BREAK
011  Pisces......... Neptune, your ruler, is strongly
     aspected
012  raising controversy in financial affairs.
013  Make time for checking accounts.
014  .BREAK
015  Aries.......... An edgy phase if you are relying on the
     co-operation of companions.
016  .INPUT
017  Goods and services might not come up to scratch.
```

Giving a prompt, at the terminal:

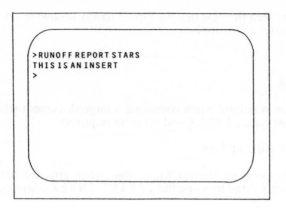

Figure 11.5

Which results in the output:

```
                       CHAPTER 1

                  THE DAILY PREDICTIONS
-----------------------------------------------------
:              The Horror Scope for Today             :
-----------------------------------------------------
Aquarius........ A bright future ahead, with an
expansion of ambitions, and plenty of social
opportunities. You'll be fairly unruffled by today's
restless conditions.
Pisces.......... Neptune, your ruler, is strongly
aspected raising controversy in financial affairs.
Make time for checking accounts.
Aries........... An edgy phase if you are relying on
the co-operation of companions. THIS IS AN INSERT
Goods and services might not come up to scratch.
```

.JUSTIFY or .J

As each line is filled, **.JUSTIFY** makes sure that each margin has a character flush against it, as seen in all the examples so far. As a result, spaces are inserted giving uneven text. This is similar to the technique used in a newspaper with justified columns.

. L E F T M A R G I N n

The left margin indicates the number of spaces that need to be indented from the edge of the paper. In the case of item STARS the left margin has not been set, so has defaulted to zero. The left margin and the line length when added together must not exceed the maximum number of characters allowed across the page. Again, in our example, the page width has defaulted to 70. By altering the format line at the beginning of the item STARS a margin can be created.

```
        STARS
001   .* TODAY'S HORROR SCOPE !!
002   .BP.LINE LENGTH 55.J.PARAGRAPH 4.LEFT MARGIN 10
007   .CENTER
008   .CHAPTER THE DAILY PREDICTIONS
009   .BOX 6,55.CENTER
010   The Horror Scope for Today
011   .BOX
012   Aquarius..... A bright future ahead, with an expansion of
        ambitions, and plenty of social opportunities. You'll be
        fairly unruffled by today's
014  restless conditions.
015  .BREAK
```

Giving:-

```
                     CHAPTER1

                 THE DAILY PREDICTIONS

      -------------------------------------------------
      :            The Horror Scope for Today          :
      -------------------------------------------------
      Aquarius........ A bright future ahead, with an
      expansion of ambitions, and plenty of social
        opportunities. You'll be fairly unruffled by today's
        restless conditions.
```

10

.LOWER CASE or .LC

All letters are converted into lower case. Self explanatory really!

```
      STARS
001   .* TODAY+S HORROR SCOPE !!
002   .BP.LINE LENGTH 55.J.PARAGRAPH 4.LEFT MARGIN 10.LC
003   .CENTER
004   .CHAPTER THE DAILY PREDICTIONS
005   .BOX 6,55.CENTER
006   The Horror Scope for Today
007   .BOX
008   Aquarius........ A bright future ahead, with an expansion
      of ambitions, and plenty of social opportunities. You'll
      be fairly unruffled by today's
009   restless conditions.
```

```
                        CHAPTER 1

                  THE DAILY PREDICTIONS

      ----------------------------------------------------
      :            The horror scope for today           :
      ----------------------------------------------------
      aquarius........ A bright future ahead, with an
      expansion of ambitions, and plenty of social
      opportunities. You'll be fairly unruffled by today's
      restless conditions.
      Pisces.......... Neptune, your ruler, is strongly
      aspected raising controversy in financial affairs.
```

10

As can be seen, the first letter of a sentence is still a capital letter. The text inside the box has been converted into lower case, and as a result "aquarius" is not considered to be the beginning of a sentence.

.LPTR

The output is sent to the line printer rather than to the screen when the runoff command is issued.

.NOJUSTIFY

The justify command in the opening format line is reset, giving output of ragged right hand margin.

```
        STARS 001 . * TODAY'S HORROR SCOPE !!
002  .BP.LINE LENGTH 55.PARAGRAPH 4.LEFT MARGIN 10
003  .NOJUSTIFY
008  .CENTER
009  .CHAPTER THE DAILY PREDICTIONS
010  .BOX 6,55.CENTER
011  The Horror Scope for Today
012  .BOX
013  Aquarius..... A bright future ahead, with an expansion of
     ambitions, and plenty of social opportunities. You'll be
     fairly unruffled by today's
015  restless conditions.
```

Giving:-

CHAPTER 1

THE DAILY PREDICTIONS

```
-------------------------------------------------
:           The Horror Scope for Today          :
-------------------------------------------------
Aquarius....... A bright future ahead, with an
expansion of ambitions, and plenty of social
opportunities. You'll be fairly unruffled by today's
restless conditions.
```

10

As can be seen, only one space is left between words, except at the end of a sentence when two spaces are left. The words are no longer spaced so that the line starts and ends flush against the two margins.

.PAGE NUMBER n

The page number is automatically incremented at each .BP command or automatic page throw. At the beginning of each document the 'n' is set to 1 and incremented from there on.

.PAPER LENGTH nn

The length of the form being used can be varied, by using the .PAPER LENGTH command. As a default the paper length is set to 66, the standard number of lines that can be printed on continuous stationery. Often for statements, special reports or letters the length needed is only 55, which is when you use this command.

.PARAGRAPH n

This command starts a new paragraph any time that the first character on a line is a space. An optional number may follow the command to indicate the number of spaces the paragraph is to be indented from the left hand margin. A gap of one blank line is also inserted into the text.

```
        STARS
001  .* TODAY'S HORROR SCOPE !!
002  .BP.LINE LENGTH 55.J..PARAGRAPH 4.LEFT MARGIN 10
003  .CENTER
004  .CHAPTER THE DAILY PREDICTIONS
005  .BOX 6,55.CENTER
006  The Horror Scope for Today
007  .BOX
008  Aquarius....... A bright future ahead, with an expansion of
     ambitions, and plenty of social opportunities. You'll be
     fairly unruffled by today's
009  restless conditions.
010  .BREAK
011  Pisces..... Neptune, your ruler, is strongly aspected
```

```
---------------------------------------------------
:             The Horror Scope for Today          :
---------------------------------------------------

Aquarius.......  A bright future ahead, with an expansion
                 of ambitions, and plenty of social
                 opportunities.   You'll be fairly unruffled
                 by today's restless conditions.
```

.PRINT

The line of text following the .PRINT command is output to the user's terminal. (i.e. the terminal that the runoff command was originally issued from.)

```
      STARS
001   .* TODAY'S HORROR SCOPE !!
002   .BP.LINE LENGTH 55.J.PARAGRAPH 4.LEFT MARGIN 10
007   .CENTER
008   .CHAPTER THE DAILY PREDICTIONS
009   .BOX 6,55.CENTER
010   The Horror Scope for Today 011 .BOX
012   .PRINT
013   Aquarius....... A bright future ahead, with an expansion
      of ambitions, and plenty of social opportunities. You'll
      be fairly unruffled by today's
015   restless conditions.
```

This will result in the prediction for Aquarius being output on screen, but excluded from a print-out.

CHAPTER 1

THE DAILY PREDICTIONS

```
-------------------------------------------------
:              Horror Scope for Today           :
-------------------------------------------------
```

```
Pisces......... Neptune, your ruler, is strongly
aspected raising controversy in financial affairs.
Make time for checking accounts.

Aries......... An edgy phase if you are relying on
```

.READNEXT

This, as indicated earlier, is used in conjunction with the .CHAIN command. .READNEXT reads the next piece of data in a list, which enables data to be inserted in a standard letter, giving a personal touch. Let's look at a complete example. Here is the runoff item:

```
       LETTER
001    .*This is a standard letter for WHICH COMPUTER?
002    .LEFT MARGIN 10 BP
003    .J
004    .PARAGRAPH 5
005    Dear
006    .READNEXT
007    We are pleased to announce that we will be exhibiting
       on our own stand at WHICH COMPUTER? SHOW.
008    We have pleasure in inviting you to visit us and enclose
       two tickets for your use.
009    You will find us on the ground floor, adjacent to the
       bar area.
010    We look forward to seeing you there.
011    .SK 2
012    Yours faithfully,
013    .SK 6
014    N. Kitt
015    .BREAK
016    For and on behalf of
017    .BREAK
018    MEGA COMPUTER SYSTEMS.
019    .CHAIN LETTER
```

In the above item a letter is being written to each potential customer, asking them to attend the WHICH COMPUTER? SHOW. The READNEXT command will read from an available file the potential customer's name and insert it into the text. The .CHAIN command starts the production of another letter if a piece of data is still available in the 'read' list.

The 'read' list is obtained by using the SSELECT verb found in Access. To select the name of each potential client, found on the CONTACT file, the following would be entered at TCL:

SSELECT CONTACT NAME

RUNOFF REPORT LETTER

The dictionary item NAME would select the name of each potential client from the file CONTACT, and make a list of them. The list may consist of:

Mr A Jackett
Mr P Harris
Mr M Bone

In which case three letters will be produced.

168

Dear Mr P Harris

We are pleased to announce that we will be exhibiting on our own stand at WHICH COMPUTER? SHOW.

We have pleasure in inviting you to visit us and enclosed two tickets for your use.

You will find us on the ground floor, adjacent to the bar area.

We look forward to seeing you there.

Yours faithfully,

N. Kitt
For and on behalf of
MEGA COMPUTER SYSTEMS

Dear Mr Jackett

We are pleased to announce
COMPUTER? SHOW.

We have pleasure in inviting you to visit us a

You will find us on the ground floor, adjacent to the b

Yours faith

N. Kitt
For a
ME

Dear Mr M Bone

We are pleased to announce that we will be exhibiting on our own stand at WHICH COMPUTER? SHOW.

We have pleasure in inviting you to visit us and enclose two tickets for your use.

You will find us on the ground floor, adjacent to the bar area.

We look forward to seeing you there.

Yours faithfully,

N. Kitt
For and on behalf of
MEGA COMPUTER SYSTEMS.

.SECTION

This is used in conjunction with the .CHAPTER command, allowing section
headings to appear in the contents list.

.SET TABS n,n,n.....

This sets up automatic tab stops, as found on any modern typewriter. Any
previous tabs that may have been set will be cancelled. Tabs only work in
NOFILL mode The tabs are activated by using the symbols> and < within
the text.

```
        STARS
001   .*TODAY'S HORROR SCOPE !!
002   .BP.LINE LENGTH 55.J.PARAGRAPH 4.LEFT MARGIN 10
003   .CENTER
004   .CHAPTER THE DAILY PREDICTIONS
005   .BOX 6,55.CENTER
006   The Horror Scope for Today
007   .BOX
008   A>q>u>a>r>i>u>s........A bright future ahead,
      with an expansion of ambitions, and plenty of
      social opportunities.
      You'll be fairly unruffled by today's
009   restless conditions.



                    CHAPTER 1

              THE DAILY PREDICTIONS
      --------------------------------------------------
      :             The Horror Scope for Today          :
      --------------------------------------------------
      A    q    u    a    r    i    u    s.......A bright future ahead,
      with an expansion of ambitions, and plenty of social
      opportunities. You'll be fairly unruffled by today's
      restless conditions.
```

.SKIP n

A break in the text is actioned and then 'n' blank lines are left blank before resuming the output of text. This can be seen in the document LETTER in the **.READNEXT** example. **.SK 6** outputs six blank lines, to leave space for a signature

---

.STANDARD

This automatically sets up a whole series of formatting commands. The settings are:

```
.CS
.FILL
.J
.UC
.LEFT MARGIN 0
.HEADING
.FOOTING
.PARAGRAPH 5
.LINE LENGTH 70
```

```
      STARS
001 .* TODAY'S HORROR SCOPE !!
002 .STANDARD
003 .CENTER
004 .CHAPTER THE DAILY PREDICTIONS
005 .BOX 6,55 .CENTER
006 The Horror Scope for Today
007 .BOX
008  Aquarius...... A bright future ahead, with an expansion of
      ambitions, and plenty of social opportunities. You'll be
      fairly unruffled by today's
```

THE DAILY PREDICTIONS

```
---------------------------------------------------
:            The Horror Scope for Today            :
---------------------------------------------------
Aquarius.......A bright future ahead, with an
expansion of ambitions, and plenty of social
opportunities. You'll be fairly unruffled by today's
restless conditions.
Pisces.........Neptune, your ruler, is strongly
```

.UC

Runoff is put into UPPER CASE mode as seen in the example for
.STANDARD

Appendix A
Summary of TCL Commands

Non Referencing Verbs

ADDD
This verb adds together two decimal numbers and displays the result on the terminal screen in decimal.

ADDX
This verb adds together two hexadecimal numbers and displays the result in hexadecimal.

BLOCK-PRINT
Outputs block letters of text on the terminal or the printer. For example the command

BLOCK-PRINT "ABC" would be output:

```
    A      BBBBBB      CCCC
   AAA     BB    BB   CC    CC
  AA AA    BB    BB   CC
 AA    AA  BBBBBB     CC
 AAAAAAA   BB    BB   CC
 AA    AA  BB    BB   CC    CC
 AA    AA  BBBBBB      CCCC
```

CHARGES
This verb displays the total time that a user has used the machine, as well as the usage of the CPU.

CHOO-CHOO
A picture of Casey Jones' train is displayed!

CREATE-FILE
Creates a new file name and sets up all the necessary pointers.

DIVD
Two decimal numbers are divided and the result is displayed in decimal.

DIVX
Divide two hexadecimal numbers and display the result in hexadecimal.

ECHO-ON/OFF	An on/off switch which, when in the ON position, displays every character entered from the keyboard on the screen.
LISTFILES	All the files of the account the user is currently logged onto are listed in tabular format.
LISTPEQS	A listing of the spooler information is produced.
LISTPROCS	Outputs all the procedures (i.e. all items for which attribute 1 contains the letters "PQ") in a named dictionary. Will automatically default to the user account master dictionary.
LISTUSERS	Output of information about who is currently using the machine: line number, time of logon, date of logon, and the account being used.
MSG	Sending of messages to a single user, a group of users or all users.
OFF	This will terminate the use of an account taking the user back to the logon prompt.
SLEEP	Further processing is halted while the machine takes as many winks as are specified in seconds.
SP-ASSIGN	Makes ready the printer for receiving output.
SP-CLOSE	Reverses the previous statement (SP-ASSIGN).
SP-STAT us	Displays the current status of all the devices used by the spooler.
T-ATT	Attaches the tape unit ready for reading from or writing to a loaded tape.
T-FWD	The attached tape is moved forward to the next end of file mark or skips a specified number of records.
T-DUMP	Dumps to magnetic tape the items specified after the verb.
T-EOD	Move the tape forward to the end of the data.
T-READ	Read a block of data from the loaded tape.

TERM	This verb sets the terminal and printer characteristics.
TIME	Displays the current time and date on the user's terminal.
WHAT	Outputs system status and configuration.
WHO	Outputs the account that the terminal is currently logged onto.

Referencing Verbs

BASIC	Calls the Pick DATA/BASIC compiler into action.
CATALOG	Creates an entry in the current account's master dictionary of the specified program.
CLEAR-FILE	The data section of the.specified file is cleared completely.
COPY	Copies a specified file to another file in the same account or, by using a 'Q' pointer, copies a file to another account.
CREATE-FILE	Creates a new file of the specified name in the account which the user is currently logged onto.
DELETE-FILE	Deletes the file and removes all evidence of its existence.
EDIT	This verb enters the editor, allowing alteration or creation of any item in any file that the user is authorised to use.
GROUP	Outputs hashing information on a specified file.
ISTAT	Outputs hashing information about the distribution based upon the current modulo and separation of the named file.
ITEM	Outputs the base frame identification number of the group which the specified item hashes. Also a list of all other items that are contained in that group.
RUN	To execute a compiled DATA/BASIC program.

RUNOFF	To output to screen or to printer a document created with the RUNOFF processor.

Access Vocabulary

Verbs

COPY-LIST	This verb allows the user to copy a saved selected list to the terminal, to another selected list, or to an item in a file.
EDIT-LIST	The EDIT-LIST verb allows the editing of a saved selected list.
QSELECT	Allows the creation of a select list from attributes in an item or items in a file.
COUNT	The verb COUNT will simply give the result of counting all the items in a file which meet any given condition specified in the rest of the command. The most basic form of the command is COUNT VEHICLE which will count the number of customer items in the file VEHICLE. The command

LIST CUSTOMERS WITH DISCOUNT GT
"10" AND WITH LOCATION "BUCKS"

will return the number of records which give the specified criteria.

DELETE-LIST	When a list of selected items from a file has been saved a pointer to that selected list has been created. The delete-list verb removes that pointer and frees the space in storage which was used to hold the list.
GET-LIST	When a list of selected items from a file has been saved on disk, this verb is used to retrieve that list. When it is retrieved, a message is output to the terminal, giving the number of items that are present on the saved list. Once this verb has been issued any of the processors may use the information held in the special list. This statement is mostly used in PROCEDURES for passing data to BASIC programs or printing labels, using the LABEL command.

HASH-TEST	This is more of a technical verb, used for determining the best size and shape for a file. It shows how any or all of the items in a file would hash into groups. The verb allows the user to enter several different file sizes and to see how the machine would organise the frames and groups. Many machines have a graphical representation of the results.
ISTAT	Again a technical verb, which provides a file hashing histogram for the selected items in a selected file, as well as an item count, the total number of bytes in all the items that have been tested, the average number of bytes per item and the average number of items per group. On the surface, this verb does not seem very useful, but is invaluable for calculating how much disk space may be required in the future. It also shows, to the experienced eye, how well the file space is being utilized. It may be that the file sizes are affecting the efficiency of the machine. Not often used on a day to day basis, but the sort of verb a technical guru will use to impress a potential purchaser.
LIST	This is the simplest, and probably the most used, Access verb. LIST CUSTOMERS will give a display on the terminal from which the request was issued with a display of all the items held on the file CUSTOMERS. Automatically a predetermined selection of attributes are displayed from every item. Other combinations of output can be specified by using the data dictionary definitions that have been set up for the file in question.
LIST-ITEM	This verb combines the format of the COPY command with the selection powers of Access. The same type of format is used as for the LIST or SORT verbs, except that no output specifications are given, as all the items requested are printed on the terminal or line printer, just as the COPY verb would produce them, complete with three digit line numbers on the left of each line. Heading and footing text can be used as well as selection criteria (LT, GT, EQ, and so forth).

LIST-LABEL

This facility enables the printing of standard labels. The command has the same effect on the data as the LIST command, except the output is formatted into a label shape and size. After issuing the LIST-LABEL command, the operator is prompted at the screen for a number of pieces of information, which includes:

1. Number of labels across a page.

2. Number of possible print lines on each label.

3. Number of blank lines between each label.

4. Number of spaces the display is to be indented (from the left margin).

5. Maximum number of characters across the label that can be printed.

6. The number of spaces between the labels (across the page).

All this information is necessary because sheets of labels vary enormously from company to company. Although very time consuming to work out for the first time, once done this command is very easy and useful to use. Also the labelling commands should not be used straight from the terminal as the answers to the questions get forgotten, or the person who knows the answers is on holiday. This type of complex command should be placed in a procedure for instant hassle-free use.

REFORMAT

The REFORMAT verb is equivalent to a LIST verb except that the resulting output is directed to magnetic tape or another file already set up in the system, rather than to the terminal or line printer. The most common use for this verb is to use the data in another file for updating parts of the database.

SAVE-LIST

This verb provides the facility to make a permanent saved list of a temporary list produced by the SELECT, SSELECT, and QSELECT verbs. These permanent lists are made available by the GET-LIST verb, and deleted by DELETE-LIST. If a SAVE-LIST is entered at TCL it must follow immediately after a SELECT or SSELECT command which generated the required list.

SELECT

The SELECT verb gives the facility to pick out a set of items or attributes from any given file and generate a list which is temporarily stored. The next command entered at TCL (or the next instruction in a procedure) will act upon this temporary list rather than the entire database. SELECT has exactly the same actions on the required file as the LIST command, with the difference that the data is not displayed but stored. These lists are available to the different parts of the Pick operating system and can be used by BASIC, ACCESS, RUNOFF, and the SAVE-LIST verb.

SORT

The verb SORT gives basically the same output as LIST but in addition the items may be displayed sorted in various ways.

SORT CUSTOMERS

will give the same output as LIST CUSTOMERS except the output will be displayed in ascending order of value of the item identifier. An ascending sort on values of any other field is achieved by including in the command a modifier followed by the item name that needs to be sorted.

SORT CUSTOMERS BY SALESMAN

will give a display of all the customers sorted alphabetically by the salesman's name. A descending sort may be produced by using the modifier BY-DSND:

SORT CUSTOMERS BY-DSND SALESMAN

Up to 15 of these sort keys may be used, producing a sort within a sort within a sort......

SORT-ITEM

This verb has the same functions as LIST-ITEM with the exception that the items are sorted rather than just listed. For a more detailed explanation see LIST-ITEM.

SORT-LABEL	This verb gives the same output as the SORT verb except that the data is displayed in label format. See LIST-LABEL for more information.
SREFORMAT	Again, the REFORMAT verb with a sort rather than a list function.
SSELECT	The SELECT verb with a sort option rather than merely a list function.
STAT	The verb STAT will give the total of a single item (as in SUM), and the average. For example:

STAT VEHICLE COST WITH MAKE.
NAME = "BRITISH LEYLAND"

This will give the total cost of maintenance of British Leyland vehicles as well as the average amount spent on each of the British Leyland vehicles in the fleet.

SUM	The verb SUM will give the total of the values of a single attribute from all the attributes in the named file, and/or which meet any conditions specified in the rest of the command, for example:

SUM CUSTOMER DISCOUNT

This will return the total of the discount field for all the items in the file. The command:

SUM VEHICLE COST WITH MAKE.NAME
= "BRITISH LEYLAND"

will return the sum of the records whose make name item contains the string of characters "BRITISH LEYLAND"

T-DUMP	This verb deals with dumping data from the database to magnetic tape. Selection criteria may be used but output formatters may not (such as totals and breaks in the listings). The tape unit has to be made ready for the Pick machine by "attaching" it to the processor before it will operate.

T-LOAD	This verb fetches data from a magnetic tape, doing the reverse of the verb T-DUMP. Only data which has been written to the tape using the T-DUMP verb can be retrieved using the T-LOAD facility.

Modifiers and output formatters for the Access verbs

BREAK-ON	This modifier is used to give a more readable sectioned listing. Rather than having one continuous piece of paper, the data can be split up into sections. Each time the value of the specified attribute changes, a break in the listing occurs. This feature is usually only used in conjunction with the sort verb.

SORT CUSTOMER BY SALESMAN
BREAK-ON SALESMAN

If the break attribute name is followed by text in double quotes, the text specified will be printed on each line where the break in the printing occurs.

BY	This tells the processor which attribute is to be the sort key.

SORT CUSTOMERS BY NAME

The following attribute is the criteria by which the sort is to take place. Only used with the SORT verb.

BY-DSND	Specifies that the sort is to be in descending order rather than in default value of ascending order.
BY-EXP	Sorts by exploding attribute values. This is for use with multi-valued attributes. The result is multiple lines for each item, sorted in ascending order.
BY-EXP-DSND	The same as for BY-EXP, multivalue attributes sorted, but the order is descending rather than ascending.
COL-HDR-SUPP	In every Access command a time and date heading is automatically output. This command suppresses the time and date headings as well as

the column headings for each of the attributes and the end of list message.

DBL-SPC This output formatter causes an extra line to be inserted between each item, to double space a listing, making it easier to read, mark and write comments on.

DET-SUPP This suppresses all detail lines when used with TOTAL or BREAK-ON. Only subtotal, grand-total and break lines are displayed. This command allows summary information to be output exclusively, rather than all the individual items in a file. Particularly useful for accounting purposes.

DICT This specifies that the dictionary portion of the file is to be listed or sorted as opposed to the data file. The processor assumes that the data portion is being looked at, so if you want anything else, specify it.

EACH See EVERY as these two verbs are interchangeable.

EVERY This modifier is for use with multi valued fields. When selection criteria are being made, it makes sure that every value in a multi-valued attribute meets those specified criteria. Without each of the multivalues being true the item cannot be true. If this modifier is not used, and just one of the multivalues matches the criterion then a successful match is presumed, which can lead to misleading information. Much care needs to be taken over multivalue attributes.

FOOTING The same as a HEADING except at the bottom of a page. See HEADING for more detail.

GRAND-TOTAL This modifier outputs text on a total line. An example is:

```
SORT CUSTOMERS TOTAL DISCOUNT
GRAND-TOTAL "THE TOTAL
DISCOUNT IS"
```

As with all text output, it is enclosed in double quotes. Other options which can be used with this include underlining all the total fields in the ACCESS statement, and forced new pages.

HDR-SUPP	This suppresses the time and date information which is output automatically at the top of every page of every ACCESS report.
HEADING	This modifier acts on a ACCESS report to produce a heading. This is achieved by including in the command the word "HEADING" followed, in quotes, by the text that is required at the top of each page. Special options are available for inserting the current date, a file name, a page number, or the current machine time. These special options have to be surrounded by single quotes:

```
LIST CUSTOMER HEADING
"CUSTOMER INFORMATION FOR
M.BONE PRINTED FROM 'F' FILE AT
'T'"
```

The above example will give a heading containing the filename ('F') and the time and date of the report ('T')

ID-SUPP	This modifier suppresses the item-identifier from being output with the rest of the requested data. The item-identifier is automatically output unless suppressed.
IF	The word IF in an ACCESS sentence indicates that the following attribute name is a criterion for making a selection. This modifier is totally interchangeable with the WITH modifier.
LPTR	By using this the output is directed to the line printer rather than to the terminal.
NOPAGE	When output is being directed to the terminal, this modifier prevents a pause of output at the end of each page.
ONLY	This displays the item-identifier only, suppressing any display items. For example:

```
LIST ONLY CUSTOMERS WITH
SALESMAN "MARK PRIOR"
```

It is also useful for looking at the data dictionary files to see what 'keywords' exist.

LIST ONLY DICT CUSTOMERS

The above command would give a list of the names of the dictionary items present in the dictionary portion of the customer file.

TOTAL
The TOTAL facility gives the total of the listed/ selected values in a particular attribute. The TOTAL is printed at the end of the listing.

LIST CUSTOMERS NAME TOTAL PURCHASE.AMNT

In the above example there will be columns for NAME and DISCOUNT, with a total at the bottom of the DISCOUNT column.

USING
This is a special word that allows for test data or dictionary file when a database is first set up. This facility is used during system development and enhancement.

WITH
See IF.

Appendix B

Summary of PROC Commands

A   This command moves data from input buffers to output buffers.

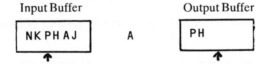

The A moves to the output buffer the string of characters being currently pointed to in the input buffer.

B   The pointer in the current input buffer is moved backward by one group of characters.

Input Buffer		Output Buffer	
NK PH AJ	B		before command
NK PH AJ	B		after command

BO
                    The pointer in the current output buffer is moved backward by one group of characters.

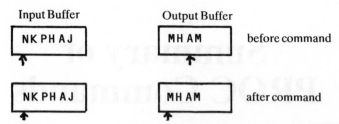

C
                    This command does not have any effect on any of the input or output buffers, but merely provides a documentary capability, helping to make the finished procedure more readable.

D
                    The current parameter (group of characters) being pointed to in the currently active input buffer is output to a terminal.

F
                    The input buffer pointer is moved forward by one parameter.

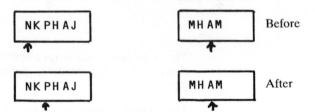

G
                    This command causes a transfer of control to a line other than the next in the procedure.

```
001 PQ
002 RI
003 RO
004 1 OHELLO, HELLO, HELLO
005 G1
006 P
```

In the above example the output line "HELLO, HELLO, HELLO" will be output on the screen continuously. (The letter 'O' is the output command). Each time the command G1 is reached the operating system goes to the line labelled '1' and repeats that line. The next line is G1, which transfers control to the line labelled

'1' and the output statement is executed..... add infinitum.

H   This moves a string of characters, forming text, from a terminal to the currently active input buffer as one parameter. For example:

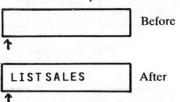

Before

LIST SALES After

IF   This is a conditional command, which introduces basic decision making capability to the procedures. For example:

IF A5 GO 15

The above statement will look for the presence of a fifth parameter (represented by A5) in the currently active input buffer.

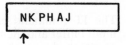

NK PH AJ

As a fifth parameter does exist (PH), the procedure goes to the line with label 15. If the condition is found to be false, i.e. there is no second parameter in the input buffer, then the GO 15 is ignored and the next statement in the PROC is executed.

IH   This replaces the parameter being pointed to in the currently active input buffer. For example, if the buffers are initially:

Input B   Output B

NK PH AJ

Then the command IH LC will produce the following result in the above input buffer:

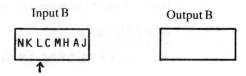

Input B   Output B

NK LC MH AJ

187

IP

This command allows input of data from the terminal keyboard into the currently active input buffer.

The command IP, with response from the terminal of MH results in:

The data that is input overwrites the data currently being pointed at, in our case "PH".

IS

This is the same as IP, except that the data is placed in the secondary input buffer.

IT

The IT command clears the currently active input buffer and then inputs the tape label from an attached tape into the input buffer.

O

O stands for OUTPUT, in this case to the terminal from the procedure. Text that follows the O is output. For example:

```
001 PQ
002 O          SCREEN HEADING
003 O          --------------
004 O
005 O          1.   PLEASE  TYPE
IN YOUR NAME+
006 I P
007 P
```

This will give the following output on the terminal when the procedure is run:

This will give the following output on the terminal when the procedure is run:

SCREEN HEADING
----
1.   PLEASE TYPE IN YOUR NAME

The '+' sign stops the cursor from moving to the beginning of the next line, giving a prompt cursor at the end of the output text.

P   Process the commands (as if still at TCL) that are currently held in the active output buffer. This, in effect executes the commands that have been stacked in the output buffer.

Other options include:

PH - all terminal output is suppressed.
PP - The output buffers are displayed.
PW - waits for the user to respond with
PW - before proceeding, after having displayed
PW - the contents of the current output buffer.
PX - returns to the TCL prompt rather than
PX - continuing the procedure.

RI and **RO**   These two commands are concerned with resetting the buffers to a null state (i.e. absolutely empty). RI is for the input buffers and RO for the output buffers.

It is advisable to use both of these commands at the beginning of a procedure to clear out any existing information in the system buffers.

S   This command, when followed by an integer value, positions or repositions the pointer in the currently active input buffer. For example, S2 will move the pointer, in the diagram below, to the second parameter.

NK PH AJ   after 52   NK PH AJ

SP   By using this command the primary input buffer is selected, and the pointer is set to the beginning.

SS   This command is as above except the secondary input buffer is made active and the pointer set to the beginning.

STON   The secondary output buffer is selected, and made active.

189

STOFF   The secondary output buffer is de-selected, and the primary output buffer is made currently active.

T   This allows the cursor to be positioned at any point on the screen, and then text via the 'O' command can be output at that point. Complex screen designs can be implemented using a combination of this and the 'O' command.

X   An immediate exit from any point in the procedure is actioned, returning to TCL.

+,-   This adds or subtracts a decimal number from the parameter currently pointed to in the active input buffer.

Appendix C

Summary of System Level Verbs

ACCOUNT-RESTORE The system has the ability to save and restore single accounts. The ACCOUNT-RESTORE allows a single account to be added, from tape or floppy disk, to the system.

ACCOUNT-SAVE A nominated account is saved onto floppy disk or tape.

CHARGES The CHARGES verb prints the current computer usage since logon as a connect time in minutes and CPU usage in "charge units".

CREATE-ACCOUNT This verb is used for creating new accounts. This includes placing a basic vocabulary in the new master dictionary.

DELETE-ACCOUNT This deletes an account and all its files from the Pick system. All users should be logged off before an account is deleted as any item in the system dictionary will be deleted.

DUMP This verb is used to display all the data contained in a single frame. The data may be displayed in character or hexadecimal format.

FILE-SAVE This verb saves the entire system, all accounts and files.

LINK-WS There are several processors in the operating system that require large amounts of workspace, or buffer area. These areas are linked when the machine is started or after a file-restore. The command allows the workspace to be attached manually from the live system. This is usually done if it is suspected that the existing links have been in some way destroyed. For example:

`LINK-WS 1-3`

will link workspace for lines one, two and three only.

LOCK-FRAME

This verb is used to hold a frame in main memory; it will remain there until the UNLOCK-FRAME verb is used.

SEL-RESTORE

This allows the selective restoration of named accounts from a system save.

STRIP-SOURCE

This is used with Assembly language program only, to remove the source, freeing large areas of disk space. The assembled code remains.

UNLOCK-FRAME

A frame locked in main memory is released.

VERIFY-SYSTEM

This checks to see if the system software is correct. Each frame in the operating system is checked, and any that are found incorrect are listed by their frame number. This verb is actioned automatically on some versions of Pick when the machine is switched on.

WHAT

This verb is used to display the system configuration, the current status of all its locks and tables, and the location of the processes that are logged on. The WHERE verb is a subset of the WHAT verb.

WHERE

WHERE displays data for all channels that are currently logged. For example:

`WHERE 'ALAN'`

will display information for all lines logged onto account ALAN.

Appendix D

Summary of the BASIC language

BASIC Functions

@(expression)

This peculiar part of the DATA/BASIC language generates terminal controlling codes when the cursor needs to be positioned other than at the left hand side of the screen. The majority of screens have a width of 72 characters, each of those characters being placed in a column. The expression:

```
PRINT @10: "HAVE A NICE DAY"
```

will result in the cursor travelling to column 10 on the screen (current line) and then printing the message contained in quotes. The line on which the output should appear can also be specified

```
PRINT @(10/10): "THIS IS THE WINTER OF OUR
DISCONTENT"
```

The specified phrase will start being printed at column 10 row 10. If you are going to draw a picture or create a whole screen full of printing, it is best to lay it all out on a piece of graph paper first.

ABS(X)   The ABS function returns the absolute value of its argument. For example:

```
ABS(5)          = 5
ABS(-22)        = 22
ABS(100-50)     = 50
```

There are no special restrictions on the range of numbers that can be used as arguments for this function, apart from the limit on the size of the numbers which can be represented by the particular computer.

ALPHA(expression)

This statement is not found in ordinary BASIC and is a true or false function. ALPHA tests for an alphabetic string. If the expression evaluates to an alphabetic string a value of true is returned (i.e. a value 1), a zero (0) is returned if any nonalphabetic characters are found in the string. For example:

```
ALPHA("LES COTTON")       = 1 (True)
ALPHA("ABC 123")          = 0 (False)

X = "THE PICK OPERATING SYSTEM"
IF ALPHA(X) THEN GOTO 25
```

In the last example, control is transferred to statement 25 if the variable X is found to be alphabetic.

CHAR(expression)

The CHAR function converts a numeric value specified by the following expression to a corresponding ASCII (American Standard Code for Information Interchange) character string. For instance,

```
EX = CHAR(33)
```

This assigns the character number 33 (an exclamation mark) to the variable EX. The argument of the function must be a integer. The command

```
PRINT CHAR(33)
```

should result in the output of an explanation mark on the screen. The CHAR function is often used in conventional computing to change upper case letters to lower case letters using a small routine. In Pick this sort of thing can be done but is not necessary due to the ease with which upper and lower case may be displayed using attribute 7 or 8 of the data dictionaries. The expression in a CHAR function must be numeric.

COL1()   Returns (numeric) column positions of the character preceding the sub-string retrieved in the most recently executed FIELD function.

COL2()   Returns (numeric) column positions of the character following the sub-string retrieved in the most recently executed FIELD function.

COS(expression)

The COS function returns the cosine of its argument. The argument is expressed in degrees. There are no special restrictions on the values of the argument of this function.

COUNT(string,sub-string)

This function counts the number of occurrences of a sub-string within a string. For example:

```
X = COUNT ('MISSISSIPPI','SS')
```
X will equal 2
```
Y = COUNT ('MISSISSIPPI','I')
```
Y will equal 4

In both these cases MISSISSIPPI is the string, and 'SS' and 'I' are the sub-strings.

DATE()   The current system date is returned in the internal format, that is a whole number counting the number of days from 31st December 1967.

DCOUNT(expression,expression)

This function counts the number of values that exist separated by a specified delimiter. This function differs from the COUNT function in that it counts the number of values by using a delimiter. This is especially useful when counting occurrences of a multivalued item. For example:

```
FRED = "ABC^DEF^GHI^JKL^MNO"

X = COUNT(FRED,'^')
```

will give the answer 4

```
X = DCOUNT(FRED,'^')
```

will give the answer 5

DELETE(expression,expression,expression,expression)

The DELETE function deletes an attribute, value or subvalue from a dynamic array. The first expression in the function gives the dynamic array on which deletion will take place. The second expression specifies the attribute, the third a specific value within that attribute (a multivalue) and the fourth a subvalue. For example:

```
OPEN '','CUSTOMERS' ELSE STOP
READ VALUE FROM 'WHITE LION' ELSE STOP
VALUE = DELETE(VALUE,2,3,1)
```

will delete the value TONIC from item WHITE LION in the file CUSTOMER, shown below.

```
     WHITE LION
001 01-428-1423
002 TONIC]TONIC\BITTER LEMON]TONIC\DRY GINGER\BITTER
     LEMON
003 30]30]30
004 0]10]12
005 ALASDAIR MORREN]PAUL HILL]MARK PRIOR
006 10 THE DRIVE CRICKLEWOOD
```

EBCDIC(expression)

This function performs the inverse of the ASCII function, converting an EBCDIC (**E**xtended **B**inary-**C**oded **D**ecimal **I**nterchange **C**ode) code to an ASCII code.

EXP(expression)

This is a mathematical function which calculates the exponential by raising the number 'e' (2.7183) to the value of the given number or expression.

EXTRACT(expression,expression,expression,expression)

The EXTRACT function fetches an attribute, a value or a subvalue from a dynamic array. The first expression in the function gives the dynamic array from which it is to be extracted. The second expression specifies the attribute, the third a specific value within that attribute (a multivalue) and the fourth a subvalue. For example:

```
OPEN '','CUSTOMERS' ELSE STOP
READ VALUE FROM 'WHITE LION' ELSE STOP
PART = EXTRACT(VALUE,2,2,2)
PRINT PART
```

will extract the value BITTER LEMON from item WHITE LION in the file CUSTOMER, shown below, and hold it in variable PART. PART is then printed.

```
     WHITE LION
001 01-428-1423
002 TONIC]TONIC\BITTER LEMON]TONIC\DRY GINGER\BITTER
     LEMON 003 30]30]30
004 0]10]12 005 ALASDAIR MORREN]PAUL HILL]MARK PRIOR
006 10 THE DRIVE CRICKLEWOOD
```

FIELD(expression,expression,expression)

This is a string handling function, which selects a sub-string from a string when given certain criteria.

```
FIELD("ABC/EFG/123/HIJ/456","/",4)
```

There are three parts to the command:

1. The original string which in our case is:

`"ABC/EFG/123/HIJ/456"`

2. The delimiting character, "/".

3. The n'th sub string that is to be found, in our case the fourth.

In the above example there are five sub strings delimited by the '/' symbol, the FIELD command will return the sub-string HIJ. The delimiters may be any ASCII characters. For example:

`B = FIELD("MISSISSIPPI","I",1)`

B will contain the character "M".

ICONV(expression,expression)

This function is peculiar to the Pick operating system as it provides the programmer with certain conversion facilities. The second expression specifies the type of input conversion to be applied to the string value resulting from the first expression.

`DATE = ICONV("01-03-85","D")`

This converts the date into internal format and assigns it to the variable DATE. DATE will have the value 6270,as this is the number of days since 31st December 1967. Also available are the time and a call to a user-written or already-provided assembler routine.

INDEX(expression,expression,expression)

This function searches a string for a defined sub- string and returns the starting column of that sub- string. For example:

`PLACE = INDEX("MISSISSIPPI","SS",2)`

Above we are looking for the second occurrence of the string "SS" in the string "MISSISSIPPI"

As can be seen there are two occurrences of the specified sub-string. We are looking at the second, which starts at column 6, so the answer that will be returned to the variable PLACE, is 6.

INSERT
(expression,expression,expression,expression,expression)

This function is used with dynamic arrays, and is part of a family of commands which includes DELETE and EXTRACT dealing with dynamic arrays. This function places a new attribute, value or subvalue into a dynamic array. For example:

197

```
OPEN '','CUSTOMERS' ELSE STOP
READ VALUE FROM 'WHITE LION' ELSE STOP
VALUE = INSERT(VALUE,2,1,2,'DRY GINGER')
```

will insert the value 'DRY GINGER', in expression 5, into
attribute 2 (expression 2). The text will be placed in the second
subvalue (expression 4) of the first multivalue (expression 3), .
The item below:

```
    WHITE LION
001 01-428-1423
002 TONIC]TONIC\BITTER LEMON]TONIC\DRY GINGER\
    BITTER      LEMON
003 30]30]30
004 0]10]12
005 ALASDAIR MORREN]PAUL HILL]MARK PRIOR
006 10 THE DRIVE CRICKLEWOOD
```

becomes:

```
    WHITE LION
001 01-428-1423
002 TONIC\DRY GINGER]TONIC\BITTER LEMON]TONIC\
    DRY      GINGER\BITTER LEMON
003 30]30]30
004 0]10]12
005 ALASDAIR MORREN]PAUL HILL]MARK PRIOR
006 10 THE DRIVE CRICKLEWOOD
```

INT(expression)

Returns an integer value for any expression.

`ANSWER = INT(47.6744)`The variable ANSWER will contain

the value 47

```
ONE = 1.34
TWENTY = 20.577
ANSWER = INT(ONE + TWENTY)
```

The variable ANSWER will contain the value 21, as only the
portion before the decimal point is considered by this function.
There are no special restrictions on the range of numbers that can
be used in this function. A popular use of the function is to round
a number to the nearest integer.

```
ANSWER = INT(TWENTY + 0.5)
ANSWER = 22
```

LEN(expression)

Finds the length of a string of characters. For example:

```
WORD = "MISSISSIPPI"
ANSWER = LEN(WORD)
```

The number contained in the variable ANSWER will be 11.

LN(expression)

This is a trigonometric function which produces the natural logarithm of the argument given. The logarithm of a number X is the power to which the base (in this case e) must be raised to produce the number X. e as in EXP is the number 2.7183.

```
LN(2.7183) = 1
```

The argument must be greater than or equal to zero.

NOT(expression)

Returns the logical inverse of its argument. Recalling that 1 = true, 0 = false, then for example:

```
ANSWER = NOT(1)
```

The contents of variable ANSWER will be 0.

NUM(expression)

The NUM function tests any given string for a numeric value, in the same way that the function ALPHA tests for alphabetic characters. The value that is returned is either a 1 (true) or a 0 (false)

```
NUMBERS = NUM("123GT")
```

The variable NUMBERS will hold the value 0 indicating that the string that has been tested ("123GT")does not consist entirely of numeric characters.

OCONV(expression,expression)

This function does the inverse of ICONV. It converts machine format data into human format for display purposes. An internally held date, which is merely a four digit number will be converted into a recognisable date. Also available are time conversions.

PWR(expression,expression)

This is a mathematical function which raises the value contained in expression 1 to the power of the value held in expression 2:

```
ANSWER = PWR(8+2,5+5)
```

The contents of the variable ANSWER will be 10 to the 100,000,000,000, or one hundred thousand million.

REPLACE(expression,expression,expression,expression,expre ssion)

This function locates and then replaces a single element in a dynamic array. For example:

```
OPEN '','CUSTOMERS' ELSE STOP
READ VALUE FROM 'WHITE LION' ELSE STOP
VALUE = REPLACE(VALUE,2,1,2,'A REPLACEMENT')
```

will replace the value 'DRY GINGER' with the text 'A REPLACEMENT', in expression 5. The item below:

```
       WHITE LION
001  01-428-1423
002  TONIC\DRY GINGER]TONIC\BITTER LEMON]TONIC\DRY
       GINGER\BITTER LEMON
003  30]30]30
004  0]10]12
005  ALASDAIR MORREN]PAUL HILL]MARK PRIOR
006  10 THE DRIVE CRICKLEWOOD
```

becomes:

```
       WHITE LION
001  01-428-1423
002  TONIC\A REPLACEMENT]TONIC\BITTER LEMON]TONIC\DRY
       GINGER\BITTER LEMON
003  30]30]30
004  0]10]12
005  ALASDAIR MORREN]PAUL HILL]MARK PRIOR
006  10 THE DRIVE CRICKLEWOOD
```

RND(expression)

This is a mathematical function which generates random numbers. The numbers are between 0 and the number specified in the expression minus one. The number contained in the expression must be positive.

```
RANDOM = RND(91)
```

The above example will generate a number at random in the range 0 to 90 inclusive, and place it in the variable RANDOM. In practice it is impossible for a computer to produce perfectly random numbers but the numbers generated are as even a distribution as is possible.

SEQ(expression)

This function performs the inverse of the CHAR function, by turning the character of a string into its equivalent numeric ASCII value.

```
ANSWER = SEQ('MISSISSIPPI')
```

The above will result in the number 77 being placed in the variable ANSWER. 77 Is the decimal number for the letter M.

SIN(expression)

This is another trigonometric function producing the sine of its argument. The result is expressed in degrees.

SPACE(expression)

This function creates a string with the number of blank spaces specified by the argument.

```
SSTRING = SPACE(20)
```

SSTRING contains 20 blank spaces. These string are invaluable for formatting a special print out

```
PRINT SPACE(20):"TAKE ME TO YOUR LEADER"
```

This creates 20 blank spaces followed by the text.

SQRT(expression)

A mathematical function producing the positive square root of the given argument.

```
ANSWER = SQRT(25)
```

The number returned to the variable ANSWER will be 5. The number supplied to this function must be a positive number or zero.

STR(expression,expression)

This function generates a string containing the first argument times. The integer is the second argument. For example:

```
ANSWER = STR("%",3)
```

ANSWER will contain a string "%%%"

```
ANSWER = STR("HELLO",10)
```

Answer will now contain the string :

```
"HELLOHELLOHELLOHELLOHELLOHELLOHELLOHE
LLOHELLOHELLO".
```

TAN(expression)

The TAN function produces the tangent of its argument. The argument is expressed in degrees. The value of the tangent function is undefined for angles° 90,270,450 degrees and for negative angles of the same magnitude. Accordingly, these values must not be presented as arguments to the TAN function.

TIME()

This function returns the string value containing the internal machine time of day in seconds past midnight.

TIMEDATE()

This function returns the string value which contains the current time and date in external human format. The format is:

```
12:34:22 05 JAN 1895
```

BASIC   Statements

ABORT{error numberparameter,parameter,...}}

Terminates a program designating the logical end returning control to TCL.

CALL name (argument list)

This statement calls a subroutine from the current program. For example:

```
CALL SUB1 (X, Y, REPLY)
```

will CALL subroutine SUB1 and execute it in place of the given statement, using, X, Y and REPLY to pass values to the subroutine.

CASE

This provides the conditional execution of a sequence of BASIC statements. For example:

```
BEGIN CASE
    CASE NUMBER < 100
    PRINT 'NUMBER IS LESS THAN 100'
    CASE NUMBER < 200
    PRINT ' NUMBER IS LESS THAN 200 BUT
    GREATER THAN 100'      CASE NUMBER < 300
    PRINT 'NUMBER IS LESS THAN 300 BUT
    GREATER THAN 200'
END CASE
```

If NUMBER = 99 then the first print statement will be actioned as the first condition has been satisfied. If NUMBER = 199 then the second print statement is actioned, and so on through the statement. There may be any number of CASE statements enclosed in the mandatory BEGIN CASE and END CASE lines.

CHAIN

This statement allows a BASIC program to execute any valid TCL command, including the ability to pass values to a separately compiled BASIC program which is executed during the same terminal session. For example:

```
CHAIN "RUN BP ABC"
```

will cause the previously compiled program ABC, held in the file BP to be executed. CHAIN cannot be used as a variable name.

CLEAR

This will set all possible variables in a program to the value zero.

CLEARFILE

Clears the data portion of the specified file. For example:

```
OPEN '','CUSTOMERS' TO EXAMPLE ELSE STOP
CLEARFILE EXAMPLE
```

When the CLEARFILE statement is executed the file that is assigned to the file variable EXAMPLE will have all its data deleted.

DATA

Stores data for future input requests when using the CHAIN statement. For example:

```
DATA X
DATA Y
CHAIN "RUN BP ABC"
```

Program ABC in file BP will be caused to start executing, when an request for data is issued. The stored data Y will be taken followed by X., and used in the program.

DELETE

Deletes a specified item in a file. For example:

```
OPEN '','CUSTOMERS' TO EXAMPLE ELSE STOP
DELETE EXAMPLE, "WHITE LION"
```

will delete the item with an identifier of "WHITE LION" which is located in the file assigned to the specified file variable in the OPEN statement.

DIM

Multiple valued variables are called arrays. Before arrays can be used within a BASIC program their dimensions must be declared by using a DIM statement. For instance:

```
DIM VECTOR (10)
DIM MATRIX (10 10)
```

This gives a one dimensional array called VECTOR with 10 elements, and a two dimensional array called MATRIX.

END

This indicates the end, physically, of a program, and must be the last statement in the program

ENTER

Transfer of control form one catalogued program to another. All variables that are to be passed between programs must be declared in a COMMON declaration in all the program segments concerned.

EQUATE

Allows one variable to be the equivalent of another. For example:

```
DM EXAMPLE (10)
EQUATE SURNAME TO EXAMPLE(3)
EQUATE FIRSTNAME TO EXAMPLE(4)
EQUATE GROSSPAY TO EXAMPLE(8)
```

In this case the variables SURNAME, FIRSTNAME and GROSSPAY are made equivalent to elements 3, 4 and 8 in the array EXAMPLE. The EQUATE statement differs from the normal assignment statement, where a variable is assigned a value by using an equals sign, in that there is no storage location generated for the variable. The advantage that this offers is that the value is compiled directly into the object-code item at compile time and does not need to be reassigned every time the program is executed.

FOOTING

Specifies a piece of text that is output at the end of every page. Also includes the output of page numbers, current time and date, and a carriage return.

FOR

This feature of the BASIC language has the following general form:

```
FOR variable = expression1 TO expression2
     statement
     statement
     statement
     statement
          .
          .
NEXT variable
```

Which in real life will look something as follows:

```
FOR COUNT = 1 TO 10
     PRINT VECTOR (COUNT)
NEXT COUNT
```

This sets the value of the variable COUNT to the value of 1, executes the statements down to the NEXT COUNT statement; increases the value of COUNT by 1; and executes the loop again; and so on, until the value of COUNT exceeds the value of expression2 (10). Then, control is passed to the program line mmediately after the NEXT COUNT statement.

FOR.....NEXT loops may be nested:

```
FOR COUNT = 1 TO 10
     FOR A = 1 TO 10
          PRINT MATRIX (COUNT A)
     NEXT A
NEXT COUNT
```

giving the ability, in the above example, to output the contents of a two dimensional array.

These loops may include branching statements which transfer control out of the loop; but loops must not be entered except by the initial FOR statement.

GOSUB

Transfer of control to a subroutine. The general form of the statement is:

```
GOSUB 25
```

which will transfer control to the subroutine starting at line 25 in the current program.

GOTO

Transfer to another statement in the same program indicated by the following statement number, for example:

```
GOTO 12
```

will transfer control to line 12 of the current program.

HEADING

Specifies a piece of text that is output at the beginning of every page. Also includes the output of page numbers, current time and date, and a carriage return.

IF

```
IF NUMBER > 200 AND NUMBER < 300 THEN
    PRINT 'NUMBER IS GREATER THAN 200 AND LESS THAN
            '300'
    GOTO 330
END
```

The above lines constitute IF statement. The IF statement can take a variety of forms, the simplest of which is:

IF condition THEN statement

This causes a single statement to be executed if, and only if, the logical value of the 'condition' is found to be true. The THEN statement can be comprised of a number of parts, finished by the END statement as seen in the above example.

An IF statement may also be provided, after the THEN clause, with an ELSE clause which contains a statement or statements to be executed if, and only if, the condition is false. ELSE clauses may also be single lined, or multi-lined (terminated by an END statement). The possible combinations of single-line and multi-line THEN ELSE statements give rise to a fair number of forms of this statement.

INPUT

This is used to request input of data from the user's terminal. For example:

```
INPUT EXAMPLE ?
```

This will output the prompt character (?) at the user's terminal. The data which the user inputs will be assigned to the variable EXAMPLE.

LOCATE

This statement is used to find the location of an attribute, a value or a subvalue within a dynamic array.

```
LOCATE('101',POST,2;VAR) ELSE POST =
INSERT(POST,2,VAR,0,'101')
```

In the above example the dynamic array called POST is being searched for the string '101' in the second attribute of each item. VAR receives answers. If the item is located then it holds the location (similar to the postcode) of the attribute, if the attribute with that string cannot be located then the location of the item if it were there is returned. If the item is not located the ELSE clause is executed, and the item is inserted.

LOOP

An alternative to the statement FOR, allowing the repetition of a number of statements a specified number of times. For instance:

```
    COUNT = 1
    LOOP
        PRINT VECTOR (COUNT)
        COUNT = COUNT + 1
    WHILE COUNT < 10 DO REPEAT
```

MAT

Assigns a value to each element of an array.

```
A = 1
B = 9 C = 5
MAT MATRIX = A+B-C
```

In the above example each element of the array call MATRIX has been assigned the value 5.

MATREAD

Reads a database item into an array, and assigns each attribute to consecutive vector elements.

```
DIM EXAMPLE (6)
OPEN '','CUSTOMERS' TO TEMP ELSE STOP
MATREAD EXAMPLE FROM TEMP, 'WHITE LION'
ELSE STOP
```

The MATREAD statement reads the file item 'WHITE LION' from the data file named CUSTOMERS and assigns the string value of each attribute to consecutive elements of the vector EXAMPLE, starting with the first element.

MATREADU

This provides the facility to lock a group of items prior to updating an item in that group. The group remained locked until one of its items is updated, or a RELEASE statement unlocks the group. The format of the statement is the same as in MATREAD.

MATWRITE

Transfers the contents of an array to a file item in the database. The reverse of the statement MATREAD.

```
DIM EXAMPLE (6)
OPEN '','CUSTOMERS' ELSE STOP
FOR COUNT = 1 TO 6
    EXAMPLE(COUNT)"COUNT*10
NEXT COUNT
MATWRITE EXAMPLE ON "RUBBISH"
```

MATWRITEU

The same as MATWRITE but with the addition of record locking.

NEXT

The last statement needed in a program loop. The function of the NEXT statement is to return control to the beginning of the loop after a new value of the variable has been computed. For an example see the description of FOR.

NULL

A non operation. Used when a BASIC statement is required, but no operation or action is needed. For example:

```
IF REPLY = "YES" THEN NULL ELSE GOTO 45
```

The above will cause the control of the program to go to line 45 when reply is not equal to YES. When REPLY is equal to YES then no action is taken, and the program control will be transferred to the next sequential statement.

OPEN

Selects a specified file for subsequent input, output, or update. Before a MATREAD, MATWRITE, DELETE, or WRITEV statement is issued the file concerned must be made available by the OPEN statement. There is no limit on the number of files that may be opened at any given time.

```
DIM VECTOR (10)
OPEN '','CUSTOMERS', TO VECTOR ELSE STOP
```

The above statement opens the data section of the file CUSTOMERS and assigns it to variable VECTOR. If the file CUSTOMERS does not exist, the program terminates message before the program is terminated:

```
OPEN '','CUSTOMERS', TO VECTOR ELSE
    PRINT "NO FILE CUSTOMERS"
    STOP
    END
```

As can be seen the END statement is used to terminate a multilined ELSE part of the OPEN statement.

PAGE

Contacts the current output device, throws a new page and prints the text contained in the most recent HEADING and FOOTING statements.

```
HEADING "ATTENTION : THE CREDIT
CONTROLLER"
FOOTING "PROPERTY OF THE GOVERNMENT"
```

The above sequence of statements will cause both the specified HEADING and FOOTING to be printed out when the PAGE command is executed.

PRECISION n

Allows the user to select the number of decimal places required on all calculations. Only one PRECISION statement is allowed per program. The n is a number between 0 and 4. Setting a precision of zero implies that all values are treated as integers. Changing the precision changes the acceptable form of a number; a number is defined as having a maximum of 'n' fractional digits, where 'n' is the precision value.
Therefore, the value

56.345

is a legal number if the precision is 3 or 4, but illegal if it is 0,1 or 2.

PRINT

The PRINT statement outputs specified data to the peripheral currently selected by the PRINTER statement.

PRINTER

This statement selects either the user's terminal or the line printer for any subsequent output. There are three forms of the PRINTER statement:

PRINTER ON - Output directed to the line printer.
PRINTER OFF - Output directed to the user's terminal.
PRINTER CLOSE - All data stored in the printer buffer (held by the operating system) is immediately printed.

PROMPT

This selects the character to be used as a prompt at the user's terminal when the INPUT statement is used. For example:

```
PROMPT "+"
```

will cause a 'plus sign' to be the prompt character. No more than one character or digit can be used for the prompt.

READ

Reads a file item and assigns it to a variable. For instance:

```
OPEN '','CUSTOMERS' TO TEMP ELSE STOP
READ EXAMPLE FROM TEMP, 'WHITE LION' ELSE
STOP
```

will open READ item WHITE LION from the file opened and assigned to variable TEMP, and assign its value to variable EXAMPLE. IF the item WHITE LION does not exist the program stops.

READNEXT

Reads the next item in a pre- selected list. For example:

```
READNEXT EXAMPLE FROM SECTION ELSE
     PRINT "UNABLE TO READ NEXT ITEM"
     GOTO 100
     END
```

specifies the list selected and assigned to the select- variable SECTION. Assigns the value of that list's next item identifier to variable EXAMPLE. If the item identifier list is empty (or if no SSELECT verb has been executed), the program will output the unable-to- read message and GOTO the statement with label 100.

READT

Reads the next item from the magnetic tape unit.

READU

This statement is functionally the same as the READ statement, except that the additional facility of locking the group from which the item is being read. A group lock prevents the access of items in the locked group by other BASIC programs using the READU, READVU, and MATREADU statements, also the update by any other program of any item in the locked group.

READV

Reads a single attribute from an item in a file. For example:

```
OPEN "","CUSTOMERS" TO TEMP ELSE STOP
READV EXAMPLE FROM TEMP, "WHITE LION",1
ELSE STOP
```

will read the first attribute of item WHITE LION (in the file opened and assigned to variable TEMP) and assigns the value to variable EXAMPLE. If item WHITE LION does not exist, then the program stops.

RELEASE

Unlocks any file groups still locked by the current program.

REPEAT

Used as part of the LOOP statement. (See LOOP)

REM

Indicates a remark. Everything following the word REM is ignored by the compiler. For example:

```
REM This statement, and all
* others that follow it,
! will be totally ignored by the
REM     compiler.
```

As can be seen, a remark statement is specified by REM, * or !

RETURN

Returns control to the body of the main program. The RETURN statement will transfer control from the subroutine back to the statement immediately following the GOSUB statement within the basic main program having the specified statement label.

```
100 GOSUB 150
*RETURNS TO HERE

        .
        .
        .
150 * THE SUBROUTINE
        .
        .
        .
        .
        .
RETURN
```

REWIND

Rewinds the currently loaded magnetic tape back to the beginning.

SELECT

This statement selects a set of item identifiers or attributes which, when used in conjunction with the READNEXT statement, is then used to access single or multiple file item identifiers or attributes from a BASIC program.

STOP

Terminates a program designating the logical end returning control to TCL. (Also see ABORT).

WEOF

Writes an end of file marker on the currently attached magnetic tape.

WRITE

Updates a file item on the database. For example:

```
WRITE "NEW ENTRY" ON A, "WHITE LION"
```

will replace the current content of item WHITE LION (in the file already opened and assigned to the variable A) with the text NEW ENTRY.

WRITET

Writes a record to magnetic tape, using the same format as found in WRITE.

WRITEU

Writes a record to the database with the group the item is in being locked.

WRITEV

Updating of an attribute value within an item. For example:

```
WRITEV "01-234-7788" ON A, "WHITE LION",1
```

will replace attribute 1 of item WHITE LION (in the file opened and assigned to variable A) with the new phone number 01-234-7788.

WRITEVU

Updating of an attribute value within an item, complete with locking of the group that the item is in.

INDEX

COPY QFILE   ISTAT fname

:TO (MD)

DELETE-FILE (fname∧ MOD, SEP)

                         | , | ∧23, |
CREATE-FILE (fname∧ Modulo, ?∧_?, Separation)

        (SAMPLES∧|, |∧23,|) [RETURN]

SORT-LABEL

COL, ROW, SKIP, INDNT, SIZ, SPACE
    4, 1, 0, 0, 16, 3

SP-ASSIGN∧=∧[FORMQUEUE]

PORTOUT∧(L,X

SP-JOBS